BIBLE
STORIES

for
MODERN TEENS

DREAMDRIFT PUBLISHING

FREE
Book

Unlock Your Free Bonus Book!

As a heartfelt **thank you** for choosing our book, we're delighted to offer you a **FREE book.**

GET THE
AUDIOBOOK

Exclusively On Audible

Scan To Download

TABLE OF CONTENTS

INTRODUCTION

In the midst of the modern world, where noise and distractions abound, the stories of the bible are still as impactful and relevant as ever before. These tales have shaped generations, guided nations, and provided spiritual nourishment to countless souls throughout history. You're invited on a transformative journey into the heart of these narratives, specially curated for today's teenagers.

Within these pages, the timeless wisdom of the Bible comes alive in a fresh and compelling way. These stories transcend the barriers of time and culture, carrying universal truths that resonate with each young person, regardless of their background. They unveil the strength of courage and kindness, explore the depths of the meaning of friendship, and illuminate the power of unwavering faith. They reveal the virtues of forgiveness, trust, and the boundless love of God.

From the shepherd boy David, who defeated the mighty Goliath, to the wisdom of King Solomon, each story in this collection serves as a conduit for moral and spiritual insights. Experience the grand adventure of Noah's Ark, witness Daniel's unwavering friendship amidst lions, and immerse yourself in the captivating tale of the Prodigal Son. Discover awe-inspiring accounts of miraculous feedings and healings and delve into parables that speak of love's inexhaustible nature, such as the Parable of the Lost Coin.

These stories are not mere narratives but profound lessons for life, aimed at provoking reflection and contemplation. They offer a deeper understanding of the profound messages embedded in the scriptures. As you engage with these stories, may they kindle a flame of introspection within you, igniting conversations and fostering a personal connection to the teachings they impart.

Bible Stories for Modern Teens is an invaluable treasury, a guiding light amidst the complexities of life. Its purpose is to empower you, the modern teenager, with the enduring wisdom of the Bible. Embrace these tales and let them inspire you to navigate the challenges and triumphs of your own journey with clarity, resilience, and unwavering faith.

So, embark on this extraordinary expedition, and let the stories illuminate your path as you navigate the complexities of the modern world.

Stories From The New Testament

4

CHAPTER 1

THE UNEXPECTED MESSAGE: THE ANNUNCIATION TO MARY

Mary's acceptance of the angel's message to become Jesus'
mother teaches us about trust and acceptance of God's plan.

Luke 1:26-38

Our story begins in the small town of Nazareth, a place barely known to anyone outside its boundaries. Here, a young woman named Mary lived, known for her gentle spirit and unwavering faith in God. Mary was betrothed to a man named Joseph, a carpenter respected for his integrity and kindness.

One day, while Mary was going about her usual tasks, her life took an unexpected turn. Suddenly, an angel named Gabriel appeared before her. Angels, as you might know, don't usually make house calls. They are heavenly beings, delivering messages from God, and their appearing often signifies events of great importance. Imagine, then, the surprise and fear that must have taken hold of Mary at this divine interruption.

"Fear not, Mary," Gabriel said, "for you have found favor with God." What a way to start a conversation! The angel then delivered the most astounding news Mary could have heard: she was going to have a son, and he was to be named Jesus. This wasn't going to be any ordinary child. He would be called the Son of the Most High, and he would reign over the house of Jacob forever. His kingdom would have no end.

What a shock this must have been! Mary was a virgin and not yet married to Joseph. Yet, the angel was telling her that she would conceive a child by the Holy Spirit. It seemed impossible, unheard of, and surely enough to turn Mary's world upside down.

"But how can this be," Mary asked the angel, "since I am a virgin?" The angel replied, "The Holy Spirit will come upon you, and the power of the Most High will overshadow you; therefore the child to be born will be called holy—the Son of God." Gabriel also told her about her relative Elizabeth, who was considered barren but was now six months pregnant. "For nothing will be impossible with God," he said.

What happened next was truly extraordinary. Mary, this young woman from Nazareth, accepted this shocking news with grace and faith. She replied, "Behold, I am the servant of the Lord; let it be to me according to your word." And with that affirmation, the angel left her.

Just imagine what Mary must have felt at that moment. She was given a responsibility like no other—to be the mother of the Son of God. She must have felt overwhelmed, confused, frightened even. Yet, her faith in God was so strong that she surrendered to His will, no matter how impossible it seemed.

Shortly after, Mary visited Elizabeth. The moment Elizabeth heard Mary's greeting, her baby leaped in her womb, and she was filled with the Holy Spirit. Elizabeth blessed Mary for her faith, saying, "Blessed is she who believed that there would be a fulfillment of what was spoken to her from the Lord."

Mary's story is a powerful testament to faith and surrender. She was chosen for an extraordinary purpose, one that would have frightened even the bravest of us. Yet, she accepted it with courage and unwavering faith. It's hard to comprehend the enormity of Mary's task. Her son was to be the savior of mankind, the one who would take away the sins of the world. The magnitude of this mission is beyond human comprehension.

However, her story teaches us that when God calls us to a task, no matter how big or small, He also equips us to accomplish it. Mary was given the strength to carry out her mission because she believed in the Lord and His promise.

Moreover, her story shows us that God often chooses the most unlikely candidates to carry out His plans. Mary was a young, unmarried woman from a small town. By the world's standards she was not someone who would be expected to give birth to the King of Kings. Yet God saw her heart and knew she was the right one for this important task.

The Annunciation to Mary is a story of faith, courage, and the love of God. From this, we learn that when God sends us on a journey, He doesn't expect us to understand everything right away. What He asks is our faith and willingness to say, "Let it be to me according to your word," just like Mary did. Remember, God doesn't call the qualified; He qualifies the called. When we surrender to His will and trust in His promises, we can achieve more than we ever imagined possible.

CHAPTER 2

THE WEDDING MIRACLE: JESUS TURNS WATER INTO WINE

At a wedding in Cana, Jesus performs His first miracle,
reminding us of God's ability to transform our lives.

John 2:1-11

Can you imagine a party where the drinks ran out? It would be like running out of cake on your birthday. That's exactly what happened in the town of Cana in Galilee during a wedding feast. This wasn't any ordinary wedding, though; this was the setting for Jesus' first public miracle.

The wedding had been going on for a few days, as was the custom back then, and the festivities were in full swing. There was laughter, dancing, food, and of course, wine. Wine was not just for celebrations; it was an everyday staple, like water. The wine ran out at the wedding. Now, that was a disaster! The host would be embarrassed beyond measure, the newlyweds' celebration would be spoiled, and a stigma would follow them all their lives.

In the midst of the bustling feast, there were some notable guests: Mary, the mother of Jesus, and Jesus himself along with his disciples. When Mary realized the wine shortage, she didn't panic or throw up her hands in despair. She turned to Jesus, confident that he could handle it. It was her faith in her son that set the stage for the miracle that was to come. "They have no more wine," she told him.

His response might seem odd to us. "Woman, why do you involve me?" Jesus replied. "My hour has not yet come." He was saying, in essence, "It's not yet time for me to reveal who I am." But Mary, like any mother who knows her child, pressed on. She told the servants, "Do whatever he tells you." She knew that Jesus would do what was right. Her trust in Him was unshakeable.

Nearby stood six stone water jars, the kind used by the Jews for ceremonial washing, each holding from twenty to thirty gallons. Jesus directed the servants to fill these jars with water. So they filled them to the brim. Then, he instructed them to draw some out and take it to the master of the banquet. Now, that took some courage! The servants could have been laughed at for serving water instead of wine. But they did as Jesus commanded.

The master of the banquet tasted the water that had been turned into wine. He didn't realize where it had come from, but he was amazed at its quality. He called the bridegroom aside and said, "Everyone brings out the choice wine first and then the cheaper wine after the guests have had too much to drink; but you have saved the best till now."

So what did we learn from this story? It teaches us several things. Firstly, Jesus cares about our everyday needs and celebrations, not just the big, life-altering events. He is involved in our daily lives, our joys and our problems. This miracle, performed in such an intimate setting, reveals a God who is concerned with even social embarrassments. He is always there, ready to turn any problem into a source of joy.

Secondly, it's about transformation. Just like the water was transformed into the finest wine, Jesus can transform our lives. He can turn our ordinary into extraordinary, our not enough into abundance, our sorrow into joy. When we bring our needs to Him, no matter how small or big they are, He's capable of not just meeting those needs, but exceeding our expectations.

And finally, it's about faith. Mary, the mother of Jesus, shows unwavering faith in her son. The servants, too, demonstrate their faith by following Jesus' instructions without question. Their faith was rewarded with a miracle. In our lives too, when we put our faith in Jesus and do as He guides us, miracles can happen.

This story, a snapshot of a joyful wedding feast, thus subtly lays the foundation for the forthcoming public ministry of Jesus. This miracle, which John describes as the first of the "signs" through which Jesus revealed His glory, is more than a mere event. It is a sign pointing to Jesus as the Messiah, the one sent by God. The one who can transform water, transform lives, and transform the world.

CHAPTER 3

TURNING THE TABLES: JESUS CLEANSES THE TEMPLE

When Jesus takes a stand against corruption in the temple, we learn about the importance of standing up for what's right.

John 2:13-22

The life of Jesus is filled with teachings that have guided people for centuries, but there's one episode that stands out due to its intense drama—the cleansing of the temple.

The temple in Jerusalem was the heart of Jewish religious life. It was where sacrifices were offered, where people prayed, and where they came to worship God. But when Jesus arrived there, he found that the temple had become a marketplace. People were selling animals for sacrifices and changing money, turning the holy place into a bustling bazaar.

Seeing this, Jesus was filled with a righteous anger. He made a whip out of cords and drove out the money changers and the animal sellers. He overturned their tables and scattered their coins, saying, "My house shall be called a house of prayer, but you have made it a den of thieves!"

This story is one of the few where we see Jesus expressing anger. But it was not an uncontrolled, destructive anger. It was a righteous anger, a response to the desecration of the holy temple and the exploitation of worshippers who had come to offer a sacrifice and pray.

From this story, we learn about the importance of standing up for what's right. Jesus did not stand idly by when he saw the corruption in the temple. He took decisive action. He stood up against the wrongs he saw, despite the fact that these money changers and sellers were likely popular with the people for the convenience they offered.

This story also teaches us about respect for sacred things. The temple was meant to be a place of worship, a place to connect with God, not a place for commerce. Jesus' actions remind us to preserve the sanctity of holy places and moments, to treat them with the reverence they deserve.

In our own lives, we may sometimes see things that we know are wrong. It could be a friend being bullied, or someone being treated unfairly, or a rule being broken. In those situations, let's remember Jesus in the temple. Let's find the courage to stand up for what's right, even if it's not the popular thing to do. And let's treat the sacred things in our lives—the things we value most—with respect and reverence.

CHAPTER 4

THE LOVING FATHER: THE PARABLE OF THE GOOD SAMARITAN

This parable teaches us about the importance of being a good neighbor and showing kindness to everyone, no matter who they are or where they come from.

Luke 10:25-37

Imagine this - you're walking down a lonely road when suddenly, you're attacked by robbers. They beat you, steal everything you have, and leave you half-dead on the side of the road. Sounds scary, right?

This is the situation in a story that Jesus told, known as the Parable of the Good Samaritan. Jesus used this story to teach an important lesson about kindness and compassion.

In the story, after the man is left on the side of the road, three different people pass by him. The first is a priest, a man who is supposed to be dedicated to God and to loving others. But instead of stopping to help, the priest crosses to the other side of the road and walks by.

The second person is a Levite, another religious person who should have known better. But he does the same thing as the priest, crossing to the other side of the road and leaving the injured man behind.

By now, you might be thinking that this story is a bit depressing. But here comes the twist. The third person to come along is a Samaritan. Back in Jesus' time, Jews and Samaritans didn't get along. They had different beliefs and usually avoided each other.

But when the Samaritan sees the injured man, he doesn't hesitate. He goes to him, cleans and bandages his wounds, and takes him to an inn to recover. He even pays the innkeeper out of his own pocket and promises to cover any additional costs.

This is where Jesus drops the mic. When he asks his listeners who was a neighbor to the man who was attacked, the answer is clear. It was the Samaritan, the one who showed him kindness and compassion, despite their differences.

So, what does this story mean for us? It's a reminder that being a good neighbor isn't about living next door to someone or even about liking them. It's about showing kindness to everyone we meet, no matter who they are or where they come from.

From this story, we learn that our actions speak louder than our words or our titles. The priest and the Levite might have talked a good game about loving their neighbor, but when it came to actually doing it, they fell short. On the other hand, the Samaritan, who was looked down upon by the Jews, was the one who truly showed love and compassion.

The challenge for us, then, is to be like the Good Samaritan. It's not always easy, and sometimes, it might feel like we're going out of our way. But remember, every act of kindness, no matter how small, can make a big difference. So, let's strive to be good neighbors, showing God's love to everyone we meet.

CHAPTER 5

WALKING ON WATER: PETER'S LEAP OF FAITH

Peter's daring walk on water with Jesus teaches us about faith and the power of focusing on God in times of fear.

Matthew 14:22-33

There are moments in life when our faith is tested, and in those moments, we find out how deep our trust in God truly is. Such was the case with Peter, one of Jesus' closest disciples, on a stormy night on the Sea of Galilee.

It all started when Jesus sent his disciples ahead of him in a boat while he went up into the hills to pray. Night fell, and a fierce storm rolled in. Waves battered the boat, and the disciples fought to keep it afloat.

In the midst of the chaos, the disciples saw a figure walking towards them on the water. Terrified, they thought it was a ghost. But the figure spoke, "Take courage! It is I. Don't be afraid." It was Jesus.

Peter, always the bold one, called out to Jesus, "Lord, if it's you, tell me to come to you on the water." Jesus simply said, "Come." And so, Peter stepped out of the boat and onto the waves. For a moment, he was walking on water, just as Jesus was.

But then, Peter took his eyes off Jesus. He looked at the storm around him, felt the wind, saw the waves, and fear seized him. He began to sink. In panic, he cried out, "Lord, save me!" Immediately, Jesus reached out, caught him, and said, "You of little faith, why did you doubt?"

From this story, we learn about faith and the power of focusing on God in times of fear. Peter was able to do something extraordinary, something humanly impossible when he kept his eyes on Jesus and stepped out in faith. But when he looked away, when he let the fear of his circumstances overcome his faith, he began to sink.

This story shows us that faith is not about the absence of fear. The storm was real, and it was terrifying. But faith is about choosing to trust in God even when we're afraid. It's about keeping our eyes on Him, rather than on the problems swirling around us.

It also teaches us about God's immediate response when we call for help. As soon as Peter cried out, Jesus reached out and caught him. He didn't let Peter drown because of his doubt. He saved him, then gently corrected him. It's a powerful reminder that even when our faith falters, God is ready to save us.

In our own lives, we might find ourselves in the middle of a storm—maybe not a literal storm but a tough situation that feels overwhelming. It might be a difficult test at school, a problem with friends, or a challenge at home. In those moments, let's remember Peter walking on water. Let's keep our eyes on God, step out in faith, and trust Him to help us navigate the storm.

CHAPTER 6

THE ULTIMATE FEAST: JESUS FEEDS THE 5,000

In a miracle of sharing and abundance, Jesus feeds 5,000 people, teaching us about the power of generosity.

John 6:1-15

There's a saying that goes, "Little is much when God is in it." This truth is beautifully illustrated in the miracle where Jesus feeds a massive crowd with just a small amount of food.

The story begins with Jesus teaching a large crowd of people. The Bible says there were 5,000 men there, not counting women and children. It had been a long day, and the people were getting hungry. But in the remote location, there were no easy options for food.

The disciples, practical as ever, suggested that Jesus send the people away to nearby towns so they could get something to eat. But Jesus had a different idea. He told the disciples, "You give them something to eat."

This must have seemed like a crazy command. The disciples didn't have the resources to feed such a huge crowd. However, they found a young boy who had five small barley loaves and two small fish, but what was that among so many?

Jesus wasn't fazed. He asked the disciples to bring the food to Him. He took the loaves and fish, gave thanks to God, and started distributing the food to the people. Miraculously, the food multiplied. Not only did everyone eat, but they had so much that there were twelve baskets of leftovers!

From this story, we learn about the power of generosity. Jesus took the little that was offered and made it into much. The young boy who shared his food could never have fed the crowd on his own, but when he gave what he had, Jesus used it to perform a miracle.

This story reminds us that we don't need to have a lot to make a difference. What we need is a willing heart. We can offer what we have—be it our time, our talents, or our resources—and trust God to do the rest. We may not see our efforts multiply in a physical sense as the loaves and fishes did, but we can trust that God will use our small contributions in ways we may not even realize.

Jesus' compassion in this story also stands out. He could have sent the people away, as the disciples suggested, but He chose to meet their need right where they were. He didn't just care about their spiritual hunger;

He cared about their physical hunger as well. This shows us that God is concerned about every aspect of our lives, not just the "spiritual" parts.

The miracle of feeding the 5,000 also reveals God's abundant generosity. Everyone ate and was satisfied, and there were even leftovers! When God gives, He gives abundantly. He doesn't just provide for our needs; He provides more than we need. This teaches us not to limit God with our small expectations. He is able to do far more than we can ask or imagine.

In our own lives, we may face situations where what we have seems to be too little. It might be a task at school that feels too big, a problem at home that seems too complex, or a dream that seems too far off. In those moments, let's remember the story of Jesus feeding the 5,000. Let's bring our "loaves and fish"—whatever we have—to God, offer them generously, and watch Him do more than we could ever expect.

CHAPTER 7

THE LOST AND FOUND: THE PARABLE OF THE PRODIGAL SON

This tale of forgiveness and unconditional love unfolds as a wayward son returns home.

Luke 15:11-32

In the tapestry of human emotions, perhaps none are more complex and profound than those of a parent towards their child. Love, disappointment, pride, worry, anger, forgiveness—all these sentiments often tangle and intertwine, weaving a story that can bring both joy and pain. In one of His most famous parables, Jesus captured this human condition beautifully, teaching us about God's boundless love and forgiveness.

In the Parable of the Prodigal Son, Jesus tells of a father with two sons. The younger son, restless and eager for independence, asks his father for his share of the inheritance. Essentially, he wanted the benefits of being a son without the responsibilities. The father, albeit with a heavy heart, grants his wish, and the son sets off for a far-off country.

In this distant land, the son squanders his wealth on wild living. He's living the high life, partying, and enjoying his freedom—until the money runs out. A severe famine hits the country, and he finds himself in dire need. In desperation, he takes a job feeding pigs, a job considered degrading and unclean in Jewish culture.

As he's longing to eat even the pig's food, he comes to his senses. He remembers his father's house, where even the servants have more than enough to eat. So, he decides to return home, ready to beg his father to take him back not as a son, but as a servant.

But the story takes a turn that's surprising in its time. As the son approaches home, his father sees him from a distance. Instead of waiting for the son to come to him in shame, the father runs to him, throws his arms around him, and kisses him. The son starts his rehearsed apology, but the father cuts him off. He calls for the best robe, a ring, and sandals for his son and orders a grand feast to celebrate his return.

Now, the older brother hears the celebration and becomes angry. He's been dutiful and faithful all these years, and there was no party for him. His father comes out and pleads with him to join the celebration. He tells him, "Everything I have is yours. But we had to celebrate and be glad, because this brother of yours was dead and is alive again; he was lost and is found."

From this story, we learn about the extraordinary love and forgiveness of God. Like the father in the story, God waits for us with open arms, ready to welcome us back no matter how far we've strayed. He doesn't just tolerate us; He celebrates our return.

This story also teaches us about the dangers of self-righteousness, represented by the older brother. He couldn't rejoice in his brother's return because he was focused on his own merit. We're reminded to be careful of a "me-centered" attitude that can blind us to the joy of others.

The Parable of the Prodigal Son is a mirror held up to our own lives. We may sometimes be like the younger son, choosing our own way and ignoring God's wisdom. We may sometimes be like the older brother, focused on our efforts and missing the heart of God's love. But regardless of where we find ourselves in the story, God is always the loving Father, ready to forgive and celebrate our return.

CHAPTER 8

Treasure Hunt: The Parable of the Hidden Treasure

This story teaches us about the value of the kingdom of God and the joy of discovering it.

Matthew 13:44

Everyone loves a good treasure hunt story, right? There's the thrill of discovery, the suspense of the unknown, and the joy that comes when the treasure is finally found. In one of His parables, Jesus gives us the ultimate treasure hunt story, but with a twist—the treasure is not gold or jewels, but the kingdom of God itself.

In the Parable of the Hidden Treasure, the story is simple but profound. Jesus tells of a man who finds a treasure hidden in a field. In his joy, he goes and sells all he has and buys that field.

The man in the story didn't set out to find this treasure; he stumbled upon it. But once he saw it, he knew its worth. He recognized that this treasure was worth more than anything else he owned. So, he sold everything—everything!—to gain this treasure.

This story speaks to us about the inestimable value of God's kingdom. Jesus is telling us that the kingdom of God is like this hidden treasure—it's worth giving up everything for. When we truly grasp the value of being part of God's kingdom, we will willingly give up anything that hinders us from fully embracing it.

But what does it mean to "sell everything?" It doesn't necessarily mean we need to give away all our physical possessions, although for some, it might. What it really means is that we should value our relationship with God above everything else. Our love for God should surpass our love for material possessions, our dreams and ambitions, our comfort and convenience, and even our relationships.

From this parable, we also learn about the joy of discovering God's kingdom. Notice how the man in the story was filled with joy when he found the treasure. It wasn't a burden for him to sell everything; he was happy to do it! That's because the treasure was worth so much more than what he was giving up.

Likewise, choosing God's kingdom over other things shouldn't feel like a burden. Yes, there may be sacrifices and hard choices, but the joy of being in a relationship with God surpasses all that. When we really understand what we gain—forgiveness, eternal life, God's presence, peace, joy, love—the sacrifices pale in comparison.

So, where are we in this treasure hunt? Have we discovered the treasure of God's kingdom? And if we have, do we realize its worth? Are we willing to "sell" everything—put God first—in order to fully embrace it?

As we continue our journey, let's seek the kingdom of God above all else, knowing it's the greatest treasure we could ever find. Let's be willing to let go of anything that hinders us from fully embracing it. And as we do, we will experience the joy and satisfaction that come from discovering the ultimate treasure.

CHAPTER 9

INVESTING WISELY: THE PARABLE OF THE TALENTS

In this story, we learn about the importance of using our gifts wisely and not hiding them away.

Matthew 25:14-30

We live in a world where investing is a big deal. Stocks, real estate, crypto—people are always looking for ways to grow their wealth. But have you ever considered that you've already been given something to invest, something far more valuable than money?

In the Parable of the Talents, Jesus talks about this concept but with a twist—the investments are not about money alone, but about life itself.

The story goes like this. A man is going on a journey and calls his servants to entrust them with his wealth. To one, he gives five talents; to another, two; and to another, one, each according to their ability. Now, in those days, a talent was a large sum, of money, but for us today, it can represent the time, abilities, resources, and opportunities God gives us.

The first two servants go and work with their talents, doubling what they were given. But the third servant, out of fear, buries his talent in the ground and does nothing with it.

When the man returns, he's pleased with the first two servants. They took what they were given and increased it. They demonstrated faithfulness, resourcefulness, and courage. In response, the man rewards them by entrusting them with even more responsibilities, saying, "Well done, good and faithful servant."

But when the third servant comes forward, things take a sharp turn. This servant returns the talent just as it was given, without any increase. He let his fear dictate his actions and did nothing with what he had been entrusted. The master is not pleased with him and takes away his talent, giving it to the one who has ten talents.

From this story, we learn the importance of using and multiplying the gifts God has given us. Just like the first two servants, we are called to take what we've received— our abilities, time, resources, and opportunities—and invest them wisely for God's kingdom.

This is not about achieving massive success or becoming famous. Instead, it's about faithfully using what we have for God's purposes, whether it's our ability to encourage others, our time spent volunteering, or our resources shared with those in need.

We also learn from the third servant's mistake. Fear held him back from doing anything with his talent. Fear of failure, fear of what others may think, fear of losing what he had. But by doing nothing, he missed the opportunity to increase what he had been given.

So, let's not be like the third servant, paralyzed by fear and doing nothing with our gifts. Let's take risks for God's kingdom, knowing that He doesn't expect us to be perfect but to be faithful. And as we do, we'll hear those beautiful words, "Well done, good and faithful servant."

In our journey, let's remember the Parable of the Talents. Let's invest wisely what we've been given, and not bury our gifts out of fear. And let's look forward to the day when we can present to God all that we've done with what He's entrusted to us.

CHAPTER 10

A GRATEFUL LEPER: THE POWER OF GRATITUDE

When only one healed leper returns to thank Jesus, we learn about the importance of expressing gratitude.

Luke 17:11-19

Jesus' time on earth was marked by powerful teaching and miraculous healings. Among the multitude of these healings, the account of the ten lepers holds a special place. This story, found in the gospel of Luke, is not just about physical healing; it's a profound lesson in gratitude.

During Jesus' journey to Jerusalem, he passed along the border between Samaria and Galilee. As he entered a village, ten men afflicted with leprosy met him. However, they stood at a distance. In their desperate condition, societal laws prohibited them from coming close to others. Their bodies were decaying, they were in constant pain, and they lived as outcasts.

Spotting Jesus, they lifted their voices, calling out, "Jesus, Master, have mercy on us!" They had heard of His power to heal, and they seized this chance to be freed from their debilitating disease.

Jesus heard their cry for help. He didn't turn away from their disfigured bodies or their hopeless condition. Instead, He responded with compassion and instruction. "Go and show yourselves to the priests," He commanded.

In Jewish law, a priest had to declare a person clean before they could rejoin society after being cured of leprosy. But Jesus was asking these men to go to the priests while they were still lepers. It was a clear call to faith.

The lepers had a choice: to doubt and question, or obey. They chose to obey. As they turned to go to the priests, a miraculous transformation began. Their decaying skin was replaced with healthy flesh. They felt their strength return. Their pain subsided. They were healed!

In their joy and amazement, nine of the healed lepers continued on their way to seek validation from the priests. However, one of them stopped. This man, realizing the magnitude of what had just happened, turned back. Overwhelmed with gratitude, he ran towards Jesus, praising God loudly. He threw himself at Jesus' feet, thanking Him profusely. It's interesting to note that this grateful leper, as Luke pointed out, was a Samaritan, a foreigner.

Jesus looked at the man, his eyes filled with kindness, and asked, "Were not all ten cleansed? Where are the other nine? Has no one returned to give praise to God except this foreigner?" Then He said to him, "Rise and go; your faith has made you well."

This encounter paints a powerful picture of gratitude. All ten lepers experienced the same miraculous healing, but only one recognized the source of the miracle and returned to express his gratitude.

Gratitude is not just a polite response; it is a reflection of our faith and understanding of God's grace. It is acknowledging that every good thing we have is a gift from God. The Samaritan lepers return to thank Jesus shows a heart that recognized God's mercy and grace.

It's easy to be like the nine lepers, who, after receiving their blessing, went on with their lives, forgetting to express their gratitude to the one who healed them. Life's busyness, distractions, and even our struggles can make us overlook the blessings we receive.

Yet, the story of the grateful leper urges us to pause and express our thanks to God. Gratitude should be a daily practice, a constant recognition of God's work in our lives. It's about cultivating a heart that, even amidst challenges, can find a reason to return to Jesus and say, "Thank you."

Indeed, this story is a reminder to celebrate God's blessings, to acknowledge His work in our lives, and to always turn back to Him with a grateful heart. For in the act of giving thanks, we not only honor God, but we also affirm our faith in His continuous work in our lives. As the grateful leper showed us, gratitude has the power to deepen our faith and draw us closer to Jesus.

CHAPTER 11

THE ENCOUNTER AT THE WELL: JESUS AND THE SAMARITAN WOMAN

A chance meeting at a well changes a woman's life, showing us that everyone deserves compassion and respect.

John 4:4-42

Meeting new people can sometimes change our lives in ways we never thought possible. But what if you met someone who not only knew everything about you but also offered you something you've been searching for all your life?

This is precisely what happened to a woman from Samaria, and the person she met was none other than Jesus Himself.

The story goes that Jesus, while traveling through Samaria, stops at a well around noon. As He sits, tired from His journey, a Samaritan woman comes to draw water. Now, keep in mind, Jews and Samaritans typically didn't get along. They had different beliefs and avoided contact whenever possible. And on top of that, men generally didn't speak to women in public. But Jesus, breaking these societal norms, asks her for a drink.

Taken aback, the woman asks Him why He, a Jew, is asking her, a Samaritan woman, for a drink. This begins a conversation that would change her life forever. Jesus tells her about the "living water" He offers—a life-giving, soul-refreshing relationship with God that will satisfy her deepest needs.

He reveals that He knows about her past, the things she's done, and the struggles she's been through. He doesn't judge her or belittle her; instead, He offers her grace, compassion, and the promise of something better.

By the end of their conversation, the woman is so impacted by this encounter that she leaves her water jar and rushes back to her town to tell everyone about Jesus, the man who knew all about her, yet offered her the chance to start anew.

What can we learn from this story? First, it teaches us about the amazing love and grace of Jesus. He meets us where we are, knows our past, yet doesn't hold it against us. He offers us a fresh start, a chance to experience His life-changing love.

The story also shows us that everyone deserves respect and compassion, regardless of their past, their gender, or their cultural background. Jesus didn't let societal norms dictate who He should associate with. He treated the Samaritan woman with dignity and kindness, setting an example for us to do the same.

Remember the Samaritan woman whenever you feel that your past errors define you. Remember Jesus' words of grace and His offer of living water. And think of her when you encounter others who are different from you. Like Jesus, let's extend kindness, understanding, and respect, because everyone we meet is fighting a battle we know nothing about. And who knows? You might be the one to change their life, just like Jesus changed the Samaritan woman's.

CHAPTER 12

TURNING THE OTHER CHEEK: THE SERMON ON THE MOUNT

Jesus' teachings on forgiveness and love challenge us to live our lives with kindness and humility.

Matthew 5: 38-39

One of the most famous speeches in history didn't take place in a grand hall or a huge stadium, but on a hillside. It was given by Jesus to His followers and to the large crowd that had gathered around Him, and it became known as the Sermon on the Mount.

In this sermon, Jesus shared some of His most profound teachings, challenging us to view life and people differently. One of the key lessons He taught was about forgiveness and love, summed up in a simple, yet powerful statement: "Turn the other cheek."

Here's the scene: Jesus is surrounded by people eagerly waiting to hear what He has to say. He begins to talk about love, but not the kind of love that they're used to. He says, "You have heard that it was said, 'Eye for eye, and tooth for tooth.' But I tell you, do not resist an evil person. If anyone slaps you on the right cheek, turn to them the other cheek also."

In a world where revenge and retaliation were common, this was a radical idea. It wasn't about being a doormat and letting people walk all over you; it was about choosing to respond with love and forgiveness, instead of anger and vengeance.

Jesus was challenging them, and us, to break the cycle of hostility and violence. He was calling for a different kind of strength—the strength to control our impulses, to respond to evil with good, and to love our enemies.

But Jesus didn't just talk the talk, He walked the walk. Throughout His life, and especially at His crucifixion, Jesus embodied the principle of turning the other cheek. Despite being mocked, beaten, and wronged in every way, Jesus responded with forgiveness. Even on the cross, He prayed for His persecutors, saying, "Father, forgive them, for they do not know what they are doing."

So, what does turning the other cheek mean for us today? It means choosing to forgive, even when we've been hurt. It means showing kindness, even to those who don't deserve it. It means responding to hate with love and to misunderstanding with patience. It's not easy, and we won't always get it right, but that's the challenge that Jesus sets before us.

From this story, we learn that retaliation only leads to more pain and violence, but forgiveness can break that cycle. It's not about being weak; it's about being brave enough to choose love over hate, forgiveness over revenge. It's about showing the same kind of unconditional love that Jesus shows us. As we embrace this teaching, we can become agents of change in our families, schools, and communities, making the world a little bit kinder, one act of forgiveness at a time.

CHAPTER 13

RISE AND SHINE: THE TRANSFIGURATION OF JESUS

The transfiguration of Jesus teaches us about the divine nature of Christ and the importance of listening to Him.

Matthew 17:1-9

Imagine you're hiking up a mountain with your closest friends, an uphill climb that pushes you to the limits of your endurance. Now imagine, at the top of that mountain, you see your friend suddenly glowing with a heavenly light and speaking with ancient prophets who have been gone for centuries. This was the extraordinary experience of Peter, James, and John—the inner circle of Jesus' disciples—on a high mountain away from the crowds.

Jesus had taken Peter, James, and John to a high mountain to pray. As He prayed, something astounding happened. His face changed, and his clothes became dazzling white, whiter than anyone on earth could bleach them. This event is known as the Transfiguration.

As if that wasn't amazing enough, Moses and Elijah—two great prophets from the Old Testament—appeared in glorious splendor, talking with Jesus. Moses represented the law, and Elijah represented the prophets. Both figures were key in the history of Israel and were held in the highest regard. Their appearance highlighted Jesus' continuity with the law and the prophets and His fulfillment of God's plan.

Peter, witnessing this heavenly spectacle, said to Jesus, "Master, it is good for us to be here. Let us put up three shelters—one for you, one for Moses, and one for Elijah." Peter, in his awe and enthusiasm, was trying to capture this moment, to prolong it. He wanted to build shelters, maybe as a gesture of respect, or perhaps to provide a place where this holy gathering could continue. However, in his excitement, Peter was missing the point.

While Peter was speaking, a cloud appeared and enveloped them, causing the disciples to be frightened. But then a voice came from the cloud, saying, "This is my Son, whom I love. Listen to him!" This voice was God, expressing His approval of Jesus. The instruction to listen to Jesus underscored His authority and pointed to His unique role as God's chosen messenger.

Suddenly, when they looked around, they saw no one with them anymore, only Jesus. The divine moment was over, and they were left alone with Jesus. He instructed them not to tell anyone what they had seen until after

He had risen from the dead. The disciples, despite their initial fear, obeyed Jesus' command.

What can we learn from this unique and transformative event? First, the Transfiguration reaffirmed Jesus' divine nature, showing that He is indeed the Son of God. His radiant appearance and the heavenly voice left no doubt about His divine status.

Second, the appearance of Moses and Elijah confirmed that Jesus was the fulfillment of the Law and the Prophets. He was the one they had pointed to, the promised Messiah, the deliverer of God's people.

Third, God's command to listen to Jesus teaches us about the importance of hearing and following Jesus' words. There are many voices in this world vying for our attention, but the Transfiguration reminds us to focus on Jesus' voice above all else.

Lastly, this story teaches us about the importance of spiritual experiences in our faith journey. Like Peter, we may wish to stay on the mountain, basking in the glory of the divine, but we are called back to the valleys of life where our faith is truly tested and lived out.

In the end, the Transfiguration is a powerful reminder of who Jesus is and what He came to do. Jesus isn't just another teacher or prophet; He's the divine Son of God, the fulfillment of God's plan of salvation. Our response, then, should echo that of the disciples: to listen to Him, follow Him, and tell others about Him. As we do, we'll find ourselves changed, not on an external, transfigured level, but on a deep, heart level that impacts everything we do.

CHAPTER 14

THROUGH THE ROOF: HEALING THE PARALYZED MAN

In this story, four friends lower a paralyzed man through a roof to Jesus, teaching us about faith and the power of friendship.

Mark 2:1-12

It was just another day in the small town of Capernaum. The usual hustle and bustle had come to a halt as word spread that Jesus had returned. People flocked from all corners of the town, wanting to see this teacher who had performed miraculous deeds and spoke words of life.

Among the crowd were four friends carrying a paralyzed man on a mat. Their friend had been afflicted for many years, unable to move, dependent on the care and kindness of others. They had heard about Jesus healing the sick and casting out demons. If anyone could help their friend, it was Jesus

But there was a problem. The crowd around Jesus was so dense that they could not get their friend through the door. Imagine their disappointment, seeing their hope so close yet so unreachable. But these men weren't going to give up that easily. Their faith and determination led them to devise a bold plan.

With their friend on his mat, they climbed the stairs to the flat roof of the house, carrying the paralyzed man with them. Once on the roof, they began to dig through the layers of straw and mud that made up the roof. Imagine the scene inside as bits of the roof started to fall, then a stream of sunlight broke through, followed by the sight of a man being lowered on a mat right in front of Jesus. It wasn't a conventional entrance, but it got Jesus' attention, along with everyone else's.

Seeing their faith, Jesus said to the paralyzed man, "Son, your sins are forgiven." This caused a stir among the religious leaders present, who wondered how Jesus could presume to forgive sins, a prerogative they believed belonged to God alone. Perceiving their thoughts, Jesus asked, "Which is easier to say, 'Your sins are forgiven,' or 'Get up, take your mat and walk?' But I want you to know that the Son of Man has authority on earth to forgive sins."

With these words, He turned to the paralyzed man and commanded him to rise, take his mat, and walk. The man got up, picked up his mat, and walked out in full view of them all. The room erupted in amazement and praise to God.

From this story, we learn some valuable lessons. The first is about the power of faith and determination. The friends were undeterred by the crowd. They didn't let the circumstances hinder them from bringing their friend to Jesus. Their faith wasn't passive; it was active and persistent. They believed Jesus could heal, and their actions demonstrated that belief.

The second lesson is about the power of friendship and community. The paralyzed man couldn't reach Jesus on his own; he needed his friends. They didn't just carry his mat; they carried his hopes and shared in his burdens. They showed us the essence of friendship: to love, to support, and to help each other, especially in times of need.

Thirdly, we learn about Jesus' authority to forgive sins. This was a radical and revolutionary message. Jesus wasn't just a healer of physical ailments; He was a healer of the soul. He came to address the root problem of humanity: sin. And He has the power and authority to forgive sins and to grant us new life.

Lastly, we are reminded of the holistic nature of Jesus' ministry. He cares for our physical needs and our spiritual needs. He has power over our physical illnesses and over the sins that paralyze us spiritually.

In conclusion, this story invites us to bring our needs and the needs of others to Jesus, in faith and perseverance. It calls us to share in each other's burdens, to carry each other's mats, in a sense. And it assures us of Jesus' authority to forgive and to heal, reminding us of His compassion and care for us. No matter what roof we have to tear apart, Jesus is always worth it.

CHAPTER 15

HEALING HANDS: THE MIRACLE OF THE BLIND MAN

The story of Jesus healing a blind man opens our eyes to the power of faith and compassion.

<u>Mark 8:22-25</u>

Miracles are at the heart of the stories of Jesus. They are not just supernatural events, but signs of God's power and love. One such miracle that carries deep meaning is the story of the healing of a blind man in the town of Bethsaida.

As Jesus and his disciples were walking through Bethsaida, they came across a blind man. The man had never seen the beauty of the world, the faces of his loved ones, or the colors of the sunrise. But he had faith, and his friends had faith too. They brought him to Jesus, hoping for a miracle.

Jesus led the blind man by the hand out of the village. Then, He did something unexpected. He spit on the man's eyes and put His hands on him. He asked, "Do you see anything?"

The man looked up and said, "I see people; they look like trees walking around." His sight had been partially restored, but it wasn't clear. So, Jesus put His hands on the man's eyes again. This time, when the man opened his eyes, he could see everything clearly. His sight was fully restored.

From this story, we learn about the power of faith and compassion. The blind man and his friends had faith that Jesus could heal him. They sought Jesus out and trusted Him with their problem. It's a lesson for us to bring our problems to God, trusting Him to provide solutions in His own way and in His own time.

Jesus' compassion in this story is evident. He didn't just perform a quick miracle and move on. He took the time to lead the blind man out of the village, away from the crowd. He gave the man His full attention and touched him not once, but twice. It shows us that God's love for us is personal and attentive. He doesn't just care about our problems; He cares about us.

This story also gives us insight into the nature of spiritual growth. The blind man's healing didn't happen all at once. First, his sight was blurry, then it became clear. Sometimes, our understanding of God is like that. We start with a blurry picture, but as we keep seeking Him, things become clearer.

In our own lives, we may encounter challenges that make us feel blind, unable to see the way forward. We might be struggling with questions about our future, dealing with a difficult situation at school or at home, or wrestling with doubts. In those times, let's remember the story of the blind man. Let's bring our challenges to God, trust Him to guide us, and remember that it's okay if we don't understand everything all at once. With time, and with God's help, things will become clearer.

CHAPTER 16

THE GREAT FISHERMEN: THE CALL OF SIMON PETER AND ANDREW

Simon Peter and Andrew's calling to be fishers of men teaches us about leaving our comfort zone to follow God.

Matthew 4:18-22

Imagine a typical day at work. The familiar sounds of the environment, the routine tasks, the camaraderie with your co-workers. For Simon Peter and his brother Andrew, that typical day was spent on the fishing boat, surrounded by the sloshing sounds of the Sea of Galilee, the harsh calls of seagulls overhead, and the creaking of their weathered boat. They were fishermen by trade, their lives dominated by nets, fish, and the unpredictable moods of the sea. Their hands were hard from work, their faces weathered by the sun and the salty sea breeze.

On one such ordinary day, their lives took an extraordinary turn. The two brothers were casting their nets into the sea, probably talking about their haul or discussing where to cast their nets next, when a stranger approached them. This man, they would later learn, was Jesus of Nazareth, whose reputation as a teacher and healer was starting to spread.

Watching the two brothers at their work, Jesus issued a challenge that would change their lives forever: "Come, follow me," he said, "and I will make you fishers of men."

This invitation was far from the mundane. It wasn't about catching more fish or learning a new technique. Instead, it was an invitation to embark on a spiritual journey, to become a part of a mission larger than themselves. They were being asked to trade their nets for a life of discipleship, their fishing boat for the challenging road that lay ahead.

Remarkably, Simon Peter and Andrew didn't question or hesitate. The Bible tells us, "Immediately they left their nets and followed him." The two brothers chose to follow Jesus, leaving behind the familiarity of their work, their families, and their home. This leap of faith marked the beginning of an incredible journey as disciples of Jesus, a journey filled with teachings, miracles, challenges, and growth.

But following Jesus wasn't always easy. They encountered storms both physical and metaphorical, they faced persecution, and they grappled with doubts.

But through all the trials and tribulations, they stayed true to their commitment. They learned from Jesus, they grew in their faith, and when the time came, they stepped up to lead and spread the teachings of Jesus to others.

Simon Peter and Andrew's story is not just an ancient tale; it speaks to us here and now. Their call to become fishers of men, to leave their comfort zone, and follow Jesus is also our call.

Just like them, we might be in our element, doing what we're familiar with, perhaps even comfortable. We have our own "nets," our own comfort zones, the areas of our life that we are hesitant to step out from. It might be a familiar routine, a stable job, a comfortable lifestyle, a set of beliefs, or even a circle of friends. We all have our comfort zones, and stepping out can be daunting.

Yet, the story of Simon Peter and Andrew teaches us that sometimes, God calls us to step out of our comfort zones and follow Him. It's a call to trust Him, to dare to follow even when the path is unfamiliar or difficult. And while it can be scary, remember that just as Jesus was with Simon Peter and Andrew, guiding and supporting them, He is with you too.

Stepping out of our comfort zones isn't easy. It might mean taking on a task you feel unprepared for, standing up for what you believe in when others don't, moving to a new city for a job, or maybe even choosing to forgive someone when it's easier to hold a grudge. These moments test us, but they also help us grow.

CHAPTER 17

THE UNFORGIVING SERVANT: THE POWER OF FORGIVENESS

This parable shows us the importance of forgiving others, just as God forgives us.

Matthew 18:21-35

In the bustling kingdom of a wealthy king, a tale unfolded that taught a lesson that would echo through the centuries. The kingdom was a hive of activity, with servants scurrying about, attending to their duties and tasks. Amidst this bustle, a man named Simon, a servant of the king, found himself in a predicament.

Simon was in considerable debt to the king. In fact, he owed the king ten thousand talents—an astronomical sum of money that he could never hope to repay in his lifetime or several lifetimes over. The day of reckoning came, and he was summoned before the king. With a heavy heart and a fear for what was to come, Simon stood before his ruler.

The king, firm but fair, decreed that Simon, along with his wife, his children, and all that he owned, were to be sold to repay the debt. Simon was distraught. The thought of his family torn apart and sold into slavery was too much for him to bear. In desperation, he fell to his knees before the king and begged, "Be patient with me, and I will pay back everything."

Now, the king was a wise man, and he saw the fear and regret in Simon's eyes. He knew that even if Simon were given a thousand lifetimes, he could never repay such a colossal debt. But the king was moved by Simon's plea. So, he took an unprecedented step. Instead of insisting on his pound of flesh, the king forgave Simon's debt entirely. Simon left the king's presence, a free man. The weight of the debt was lifted from his shoulders, replaced with an almost overwhelming relief and gratitude.

One would think that having been shown such incredible mercy, Simon would go out and share this same mercy with others. But the tale takes a disappointing turn. No sooner had Simon left the king's palace than he met a fellow servant, James, who owed him a hundred silver coins—a small sum when compared to what Simon had owed the king.

Simon seized James by the collar, demanding that he pay back what he owed. James, falling at Simon's feet, pleaded in a manner eerily similar to how Simon had pleaded with the king. "Be patient with me," he implored, "and I will pay you back." But Simon wouldn't hear of it. He had James thrown into prison until he could repay the debt

Word of Simon's harsh actions reached the king. Disappointed and angered, he summoned Simon back to his presence. "You wicked servant," the king admonished him, "I canceled all your debt because you begged me to. Shouldn't you have shown mercy to your fellow servant, just as I showed it to you?" The king then handed Simon over to the jailers until he could repay his original debt.

This story, a parable told by Jesus, gives us a profound lesson on forgiveness. We are often like Simon, generously forgiven by God of a debt we could never repay—our sins. God's forgiveness is an act of divine mercy, wiping our slate clean.

Yet, when it comes to extending forgiveness to others, we are sometimes quick to forget the mercy shown to us. We hold on to grudges and demand payment for the wrongs done to us, no matter how small they may seem in comparison to our forgiven debt. This story calls us to mirror the king's mercy—to forgive others just as we have been forgiven.

It also reminds us of the consequences of harboring unforgiveness. Just like the king who withdrew his mercy when Simon failed to forgive, our unforgiveness can disrupt our relationship with God. Forgiveness is not just an emotional release but also a spiritual mandate, affecting our connection with the divine.

So, as we navigate our relationships with others, let us remember the king's mercy and the unforgiving servant. Let us remember the enormous debt of sin that God has forgiven in our lives, and may this remind us to extend that same grace to others. This is the power of forgiveness—a cornerstone of our faith and a reflection of God's merciful heart.

CHAPTER 18

LYDIA'S CONVERSION: OPENING OUR HEARTS TO GOD

The story of Lydia, a merchant who becomes a believer, shows us that God's message is open to everyone.

Acts 16:11-15

L ydia's story is not often told, but it's one that resonates with many who have experienced a transformative encounter with the teachings of God. Lydia was a woman of influence, a businesswoman dealing in purple cloth, a luxury item in the Roman world. She hailed from Thyatira, a city known for its dye works. She was prosperous, independent, and seemingly had it all.

Yet, her heart yearned for something more profound. This led her to worship the God of the Israelites, even though she wasn't Jewish. Lydia was a seeker, a God-fearer, her heart ripe for the truth of the Gospel.

One day, she traveled to Philippi, a prominent city in Macedonia. It was the Sabbath, and Lydia, along with other women, had gathered by the riverside. The riverbank was a tranquil place of prayer, away from the hustle and bustle of the city. It was here that she had an encounter that would change her life forever.

A group of men led by Paul, a disciple of Jesus, approached the women's gathering. They had planned to go to the synagogue that day, but since Philippi had no synagogue, they went where they knew worshipers of God would gather. Paul began to speak; his words flowed like the river nearby, telling the story of a man named Jesus. The story was powerful, telling of his life, his death, and his resurrection. He spoke of God's love and Jesus' teachings about kindness, compassion, and forgiveness.

Lydia listened, her heart attuned to the words that Paul was speaking. The message stirred something within her, a shift, a recognition of a truth she had been seeking. The scripture tells us that God opened her heart to pay attention to what was said by Paul. It was a divine encounter, God touching a seeking heart with the life-altering message of the Gospel.

Lydia accepted Jesus as her savior that day by the river. She and her household were baptized, a public declaration of their newfound faith. In her, the seed of the Gospel found fertile ground. But her story doesn't end there.

Lydia then opened her home to Paul and his companions. "If you consider me a believer in the Lord," she said, "come and stay at my house." It was a significant offer. In those times, opening one's home wasn't just providing a room for the night. It meant providing food, safety, and companionship. Lydia's house became a place of fellowship and a base for Paul's ministry in Philippi.

Her conversion was not a quiet, personal moment but the beginning of a Christian community in Philippi. Her open heart led to an open home, leading many more open hearts towards the message of Jesus.

The story of Lydia teaches us that God's message is open to everyone, irrespective of their social standing, gender, or nationality. Lydia, a non-Jew, a woman, a business person, was chosen to become the pillar of the Church in Philippi.

Moreover, it teaches us about the transformative power of an encounter with God's word. Lydia's heart was open, and when she heard the Gospel, she embraced it fully, affecting not just her life but the lives of those around her.

Finally, Lydia's story is about how faith leads to action. After her conversion, she offered her home for the furtherance of the Gospel. It shows us that our faith should lead us to serve others and provide hospitality and kindness.

In our own lives, we may have moments by the river, moments when we feel a deep connection to something beyond ourselves. Lydia's story invites us to keep our hearts open for these divine encounters, to listen to the Gospel, and to act on our faith. For, as in the case of Lydia, an open heart can become a channel of blessings for many.

CHAPTER 19

THE COIN IN THE FISH'S MOUTH: TRUSTING IN GOD'S PROVISION

When Jesus provides a coin in a fish's mouth for taxes, it teaches us about trusting God to meet our needs.

Matthew 17:24-27

During the time when Jesus and His disciples journeyed through the land, teaching and healing, they encountered many moments that tested their faith and demonstrated the immense power and wisdom of God. One such occasion was when they found themselves in Capernaum, facing the tax collectors.

The collectors approached Peter one day. "Does your teacher not pay the temple tax?" they asked, their brows furrowed in inquiry.

Peter, caught off guard, quickly responded, "Yes, of course." The tax collectors, satisfied with his response, left Peter with his thoughts.

Rattled by this unexpected encounter, Peter entered the house where Jesus was staying. Before he could utter a word about his encounter, Jesus asked him a question. "What do you think, Simon? From whom do kings of the earth take toll or tax? From their sons or from others?"

Peter, a bit taken aback by Jesus' immediate understanding of the situation, replied, "From others."

And Jesus said to him, "Then the sons are free."

The concept seemed revolutionary. Still, Jesus wasn't promoting tax evasion or disobedience. Instead, He was establishing an important point about the children of God's Kingdom. Yet, not wanting to offend anyone, Jesus proposed a solution to the impending tax issue. "Go to the sea and cast a hook, and take the first fish that comes up. When you open its mouth, you will find a shekel. Take that and give it to them for me and you."

Peter, though accustomed to Jesus' miracles, couldn't hide his surprise. But trusting Jesus, he did as instructed. He went down to the sea, the salty breeze tousling his hair, and cast his hook into the water. With faith, he waited. Before long, a fish bit. Peter reeled it in, and as Jesus had said, there was a silver shekel in its mouth - just enough to cover the temple tax for both of them.

Amazed yet again by Jesus' foresight and provision, Peter returned to Jesus, coin in hand. He then went to the tax collectors and paid the tax as required, all the while marveling at the miraculous provision they had received.

In this story, we learn a significant lesson about trusting in God's provision. It wasn't so much about the tax or the coin but about the disciples' faith in God's ability to provide for their needs, no matter how strange or impossible the method might seem. We see Jesus using this situation to teach about God's sovereignty, His knowledge of our needs, and His power to provide in extraordinary ways.

Even today, this story reverberates with our own experiences. There are moments when we find ourselves worrying about our needs, whether they are physical, emotional, or spiritual. But Jesus' miraculous provision for the tax is a reminder that we are called to trust God, especially when we don't understand the circumstances or can't see the solution.

In the grand scheme of God's plan, we are part of His Kingdom, and He will provide for us. This does not mean that a coin will miraculously appear when we need it, but rather that God, in His wisdom and love, will provide for our needs in the way that He sees fit. And for that, we can put our trust in Him and His provision, as Peter did.

CHAPTER 20

THE LOST SHEEP: GOD'S UNENDING SEARCH FOR US

This parable teaches us that God values every individual and will go to great lengths to bring them back to Him.

Luke 15:1-7

Once upon a time, in a world far removed from our own yet not so different, there was a shepherd named Eli. Eli was an ordinary man living in extraordinary times. Each day, he would guide his flock of one hundred sheep through green pastures and alongside quiet streams. Eli knew each of his sheep by name and could even recognize them by their distinct baas.

One day, as the sun was setting, Eli was rounding up his flock to return home. He called out to them, counting each one as they passed by. But as he neared the end, a sense of panic started to rise within him. He counted again, but the result was the same. Ninety-nine. One of his sheep was missing.

Eli was faced with a decision: should he stay with his ninety-nine sheep and keep them safe or venture out into the wilderness to find his one lost sheep? The night was falling, and the wilderness could be a dangerous place filled with predators. However, the thought of leaving one of his flock alone and afraid was unthinkable to Eli. So, he entrusted the ninety-nine to his trusty sheepdog, gathered his staff, and set off into the encroaching darkness.

Eli searched high and low, through rocky terrain and thickets of thorns. His feet ached, and his eyes grew heavy, but his spirit remained undeterred. As the moon rose high in the sky, a soft, familiar sound reached Eli's ears—a scared and lonely baa.

Following the sound, Eli found his lost sheep caught in a bramble of bushes. The sheep was frightened but unharmed. Relief flooded through Eli as he carefully untangled the sheep and lifted it onto his shoulders. Despite his weariness, he couldn't help but feel a sense of joy. He had found his lost sheep.

As Eli carried the sheep back home, he thought of his friends and neighbors. He couldn't wait to share his joy with them. Yes, it was just one sheep, but to Eli, that one sheep was as important as the rest of the flock.

Once he returned, he gathered his community. "Rejoice with me," Eli exclaimed, holding up the lost sheep, now safe and sound. "I have found my lost sheep!"

And the whole community celebrated Eli's dedication and the return of the lost sheep.

From this story, we learn about the depth of God's love for us. Just like Eli with his sheep, God values each and every one of us. If we wander away or lose our path, God doesn't forget about us. He searches for us, longs for our return, and rejoices when we come back to Him.

This teaches us a powerful lesson about how we should value each other. Each of us matters. Each of us is worth the search. Each of us is a cause for celebration. So let's remember to care for one another, appreciate each other's worth, and celebrate every individual's unique journey. Because we are all part of God's flock, and He cherishes us all equally.

CHAPTER 21

BETRAYAL AND NEW BEGINNINGS: THE EASTER STORY OF JESUS

Jesus was betrayed by his disciple Judas, crucified, and then miraculously rose from the dead three days later, symbolizing hope, redemption, and the triumph of love over death.

Luke 22-24

Long ago, in the ancient city of Jerusalem, there was a profound sense of anticipation. People from all walks of life whispered about a man named Jesus, a humble carpenter from Nazareth, who had become a beacon of hope. He had healed the sick, raised the dead, and shared teachings of love and compassion. His message? The Kingdom of Heaven was close at hand, and everyone was invited.

As Passover approached, Jesus and his twelve disciples gathered for a special meal, what would come to be known as the Last Supper. In a room lit by dim candles,

Jesus took bread, broke it and said, "This is my body, given for you." Taking a cup of wine, he added, "This is my blood, poured out for many for the forgiveness of sins." It was a moment of deep connection, but also of foreboding, for Jesus knew what lay ahead.

Among the disciples was Judas, a man struggling with his own demons. Lured by 30 silver coins and disillusionment, he had secretly agreed to betray Jesus to the religious leaders who felt threatened by Jesus' growing influence.

That very night, as Jesus prayed in the Garden of Gethsemane, soldiers arrived, led by Judas. With a kiss, a sign of friendship and intimacy, Judas betrayed Jesus, marking him for arrest.

The next hours were agonizing. Jesus, the man who had brought hope and healing to so many, was tried, mocked, and sentenced to die on a cross. As he hung there, some ridiculed him, while others wept. Jesus, in his final moments, forgave his tormentors and promised paradise to a thief crucified beside him. And then, with a final cry, he breathed his last.

The world seemed to hold its breath. The earth shook, the sky darkened, and Jesus' followers mourned the loss of their beloved teacher.

But the story doesn't end there.

Three days later, the unimaginable happened. Women who had come to anoint Jesus' body found the tomb empty. Angels proclaimed, "He is not here; he has risen!" Jesus, defying all expectations, had risen from the dead.

He appeared to his disciples, showing them his wounds, breaking bread with them, and reminding them of his teachings. The resurrection was not just about defeating death; it was about new beginnings, love triumphing over hate, and the assurance that good always prevails.

From this story, we're reminded of the sacrifices made out of love and the boundless hope that emerges even from the darkest moments. Betrayal, pain, and death were part of Jesus' journey, but so were love, sacrifice, and resurrection. When we face challenges or feel betrayed, we can look to this story for inspiration, knowing that after the darkest night, a new dawn awaits.

Remember, life's trials may test us, but with faith and hope, we can always find a way to rise again. So when you find yourself in moments of despair, remember the Easter story and know that rebirth and redemption are always within reach.

CHAPTER 22

THE EMPTY TOMB:
THE WOMEN AT DAWN

*The experience of the women at Jesus' empty tomb teaches us
about the joy and responsibility of sharing the Good News.*

Luke 24:1-12

In the dim light of the earliest hours of the day, a hushed conversation rose and fell between a small group of women. Their arms were laden with bundles of spices, and their eyes held a quiet sorrow that tugged at the edges of their weary faces. Mary Magdalene, Mary the mother of James, Joanna, and Salome were on a mission of love, preparing to anoint the body of their beloved Jesus.

Having witnessed His brutal crucifixion, their hearts were heavy with the weight of loss. Jesus, their teacher, healer, and friend, had been laid to rest in a tomb, and a large stone had been rolled across its entrance. Now, as they drew closer to the burial site, the first tendrils of unease began to weave through their thoughts. "Who will roll the stone away from the entrance of the tomb?" they asked one another.

As the tomb came into view, however, their concern turned to astonishment. The stone had been rolled away. The formidable obstacle they had worried about was no longer a barrier. They entered the tomb, their minds whirling, only to be met with an even more astonishing sight. The body of Jesus was not there.

A dazzling figure in radiant clothing stood before them. The angel said, "Do not be alarmed. You are looking for Jesus the Nazarene, who was crucified. He has risen! He is not here! See the place where they laid Him. But go, tell His disciples and Peter, 'He is going ahead of you into Galilee.' There you will see Him, just as He told you."

The tomb was empty. The stark absence of Jesus' body brought with it a profound revelation. He was not defeated by death; He had overcome it. The truth of the angel's words echoed in the hollow tomb, "He has risen." Their grief was swept away in the surging tide of joyous realization. Jesus was alive!

The women fled from the tomb, trembling and astonished. Their hearts, once heavy with sorrow, were now ablaze with the news of the resurrection. They were the first to witness the empty tomb, the first to hear the glorious news, and now, they were tasked with the responsibility to share it.

Racing back to the disciples, they stumbled over their words in their haste to convey what they had seen and heard. The tale of an empty tomb and a risen Christ was met with disbelief from some, but Peter ran to the tomb to see for himself, finding it just as the women had described. The seed of resurrection hope was sown.

The experience of these women at dawn is a lesson in joy and the beauty of being chosen to carry the Good News. They had approached the tomb, expecting to see the finality of death. Instead, they became witnesses to the miracle of resurrection. Their sorrow was turned into joy, their mourning into dancing.

The story teaches us that God often does the unexpected in our lives. He turns our sorrows into joy, our despair into hope. Just as dawn breaks after the darkest hour, the light of resurrection broke through the despair the women carried.

Furthermore, the women's story underscores the privilege and responsibility of sharing the Good News. They were entrusted with the message of resurrection, a message that they were then commanded to share with others. It is a powerful reminder for all believers of our call to share the Good News. In doing so, we participate in the joy of the resurrection, passing that joy on to others.

The women at the tomb, in the breaking dawn of the first Easter, became the bearers of the most wonderful news ever told. They teach us that joy can arise from sorrow, hope can spring from despair, and that every believer has a part to play in sharing the Good News. The dawn they experienced was not only a new day but also a new era in human history, one marked by the hope of the resurrection. Their story prompts us to carry and share this hope with a world that often walks in darkness, bringing the light of the risen Christ to all.

CHAPTER 23

DOUBT TO BELIEF: THOMAS'S ENCOUNTER WITH THE RISEN JESUS

Doubting Thomas' encounter with the risen Jesus teaches us about the importance of faith, even when we can't see.

John 20:24-29

The room was filled with a tense silence. The disciples were gathered together, still in shock and grief over the crucifixion of their teacher, Jesus. They spoke in hushed whispers, their words bouncing off the cold stone walls. It was here that something extraordinary happened: Jesus appeared amongst them, even though the doors were locked.

The disciples' grief turned into joy, their despair into hope. But one of their number was not there. Thomas, also called Didymus, had not been present when Jesus appeared. When he returned and the others told him what had happened, he found their story hard to believe.

"Unless I see the nail marks in his hands and put my finger where the nails were, and put my hand into his side, I will not believe," he said. His skepticism echoed the uncertainty that lurks in the hearts of many, the nagging doubts that sometimes accompany faith.

A week later, the disciples were again in the house, and this time, Thomas was with them. The doors were locked, but Jesus came and stood among them and said, "Peace be with you!" He turned to Thomas and said, "Put your finger here; see my hands. Reach out your hand and put it into my side. Stop doubting and believe."

Thomas' response was immediate and profound. He said, "My Lord and my God!" In this moment, all of his doubts dissolved. His skepticism was replaced by a deep and resolute faith. He had seen and touched Jesus. He had encountered the risen Christ.

This story offers powerful insights into the nature of faith and belief. It shows us that faith is not without doubts and questions. Thomas was a devoted follower of Jesus, yet he still had his moments of doubt. But doubt, when confronted and addressed, can lead to a deeper, more resilient faith.

Moreover, the story demonstrates the patience and understanding of Jesus in dealing with our doubts. Jesus didn't rebuke Thomas for his skepticism. Instead, he met Thomas in his doubts, inviting him to touch his wounds, to see and to believe. This tells us that Jesus is not threatened by our questions or uncertainties. He invites us into an honest and authentic faith, a faith that is not afraid to wrestle with doubts.

The story also underlines the importance of personal experience in faith. Thomas' faith was solidified through his personal encounter with Jesus. It reminds us that faith is more than just accepting what others tell us; it involves personal experiences and encounters with God.

Finally, the story emphasizes the blessedness of those who believe without seeing. Jesus said, "Because you have seen me, you have believed; blessed are those who have not seen and yet have believed." In a sense, this is a word for us, who live thousands of years after these events took place. We have not seen the risen Jesus physically, yet we are called to believe.

So, from this story, we learn that faith involves wrestling with doubts and finding God in the midst of them. We learn that faith is a personal journey, anchored in our encounters with the divine. And we are reminded that, blessed are we who have not seen and yet have believed. We, like Thomas, are invited to make the same confession of faith: "My Lord and my God!"

Stories From The Old Testament

CHAPTER 24

Paradise Lost: The Tale of Adam, Eve, and the First Choices

In the Garden of Eden, Adam and Eve, the first humans,
succumb to temptation by eating forbidden fruit, leading to their
awareness of guilt and their expulsion from paradise.

Genesis 2-3

In the vast expanse of timelessness, when the universe was young and bursting with radiant energy, God sculpted a paradise, a perfect haven of harmony and beauty known as the Garden of Eden. It was a place where rivers meandered through luscious green meadows, where trees bore succulent fruits, and flowers exuded fragrances that stirred the soul.

In the heart of this Eden, God crafted the first human, Adam, from the dust of the ground, breathing life into him with a divine breath. But as Adam roamed the garden, it became apparent that while he was surrounded by creatures of all kinds, he was alone of his kind. Recognizing this solitude, God, in a compassionate act, caused a deep sleep to fall upon Adam. From one of his ribs, God fashioned Eve, a companion for Adam, so they could share the joys and wonders of Eden together.

The Garden was a playground for the two, a place of pure joy, untouched by sorrow or pain. The two lived in harmony with all creatures, naming them and watching over them. They lived under just one divine rule: they could eat from any tree in the garden, except for the Tree of the Knowledge of Good and Evil.

However, in the shadows of this paradise lurked a cunning serpent, an embodiment of deceit. Seeing the happiness and innocence of the first couple, the serpent felt a surge of envy and mischief. It approached Eve one day, its voice dripping with honeyed words, "Did God really say you can't eat from any tree in the garden?"

Eve, unsuspecting of the serpent's deceitful nature, responded, "We may eat from any tree, except the Tree of the Knowledge of Good and Evil, for if we do, we will surely die."

The serpent, sensing an opportunity, whispered, "You will not certainly die. Instead, when you eat from it, your eyes will be opened, and you will be like God, knowing good and evil."

Eve, curious and tempted by the promise of wisdom, looked at the tree anew. Its fruit seemed more tantalizing than ever before. Thinking of the knowledge it promised, she took a fruit and bit into it. The taste was unlike anything she'd ever experienced. She then offered it to Adam, who, without hesitation, tasted it too.

But as the flavors melted away, something changed. A wave of realization washed over them. The innocent veil that had protected them lifted, and they became aware of their nakedness, feeling vulnerable and exposed. The profound connection they shared with the universe seemed to waver.

Realizing their actions, they hastily sewed fig leaves together to cover themselves. Their paradisiacal existence, once so carefree and joyous, was now marked by the weight of their choice.

The next day, as the gentle breeze of Eden rustled the leaves, God walked through the garden, seeking Adam and Eve. But instead of running to greet Him as they always did, the couple hid, their hearts heavy with guilt.

"Why do you hide?" God called.

Adam, his voice shaking, replied, "I heard you in the garden, and I was afraid because I was naked."

God asked, "Who told you that you were naked? Have you eaten from the tree I commanded you not to?"

The weight of their actions bearing down on them, Adam and Eve tried to deflect the blame. Adam pointed to Eve, "The woman you gave me, she gave me the fruit."

And Eve blamed the serpent, "The serpent deceived me."

The consequences of their choices were inevitable. God declared that the serpent would be cursed, forever crawling on its belly, forever at odds with humanity. Eve would face the pains of childbirth and a complicated relationship with Adam. And Adam would toil the earth, which would no longer yield its fruits as easily.

But even in this moment of profound loss, God's compassion shone through. He crafted garments of skin for the first couple, ensuring their protection even as they left paradise.

Banished from Eden and the Tree of Life, Adam and Eve began a new chapter outside the garden's protective embrace. It was a chapter filled with challenges, but also with the promise of a future. For from their lineage would come leaders, prophets, and eventually, a savior.

The story of Adam and Eve, the tale of the first choices and their consequences, serves as a powerful reminder. It tells us of the weight our choices carry, of the allure of curiosity, and the dangers of temptation. But it also speaks of resilience, hope, and God's undying love for humanity. In their journey, we see the start of our own, filled with both trials and triumphs.

From this narrative, we learn that while every choice has its repercussions, every mistake is also a step towards growth. Even in our weakest moments, when we stray from our path, the promise of redemption and new beginnings is never far. Like Adam and Eve, we might face hardships, but with faith and perseverance, we can always find our way back to grace.

CHAPTER 25

THE STORY OF CAIN, ABEL, AND THE PROMISE OF SETH

Cain's jealousy led him to commit the first act of murder against his brother Abel, but the birth of Seth to Adam and Eve symbolized hope and God's enduring promise to humanity after profound loss.

Genesis 4:1-16

In the world outside the Garden of Eden, where hardship and toil became a part of life's rhythm, Adam and Eve were blessed with two sons: Cain, the elder, a hardworking tiller of the soil, and Abel, the younger, a shepherd who tended to his flock with care.

Both brothers, desiring to offer their best to God, brought forth their offerings. Abel's sacrifice was from the firstborn of his flock, the finest he had, while Cain brought produce from his labor on the land. But while God looked favorably upon Abel's offering, Cain's was not received with the same warmth. No one knows why; perhaps it was the intention behind the gift or the quality of the offering. But this distinction ignited a flame of jealousy in Cain's heart.

God, in His wisdom, approached Cain, cautioning him about the dangerous path he was treading. "If you do well, won't you be accepted? But if you do not, sin is crouching at your door; it desires to have you, but you must rule over it," God advised. But Cain's jealousy and anger clouded his judgment.

One day, while the brothers were in the field, Cain's resentment reached its peak. In a moment of unchecked rage, he turned on Abel and took his life, marking the first tragic act of bloodshed in human history.

God, ever observant, approached Cain, "Where is your brother Abel?" To which Cain retorted, "Am I my brother's keeper?" God, however, knew of the grievous act Cain had committed and declared that the ground which had swallowed Abel's blood would no longer yield its fruits to Cain. Marked so that no one would take vengeance upon him, Cain was condemned to be a restless wanderer, forever distanced from his family and his home.

Adam and Eve, already bearing the weight of their actions in Eden, were now struck with the sorrow of losing a son at the hands of another. Yet, even in the depth of their despair, hope emerged. They were blessed with another son, Seth. In Seth, they saw not just a new beginning but also a continuation of God's promise to humanity.

Seth, whose name means "appointed" or "substitute," grew to be righteous and became the progenitor of a line that would eventually lead to notable figures like Noah and, many generations later, Jesus.

The story of Cain and Abel underscores the perils of unchecked emotions and the devastating consequences they can bring about. But with Seth's birth, we are reminded that even in the aftermath of profound loss, hope can be reborn, and God's plans remain steadfast.

From this tale, we learn the importance of mastering our darker impulses and seeking redemption in the wake of our mistakes. Life may present challenges that test our character, but it also offers opportunities for growth, healing, and renewal. Like Adam and Eve, we must navigate the tragedies but also embrace the new beginnings that promise a brighter future.

CHAPTER 26

SURVIVING THE FLOOD: NOAH'S ARK

Noah's tale of survival during the great flood shows us the importance of listening to God, even when others doubt us.

Genesis 6-9

The story of Noah is probably one of the most iconic in the Bible. Noah was a righteous man who lived in a time when the world was full of wickedness. God, saddened by the state of humanity, decided to send a great flood to cleanse the Earth. But Noah found favor in the eyes of God.

God gave Noah specific instructions to build an ark—a giant boat capable of housing his family and a pair of every kind of animal. It was a daunting task, and what made it even more challenging was the fact that it had never rained before on Earth. The idea of a flood was completely alien to Noah and the people of his time.

Imagine the scene—Noah, an ordinary man, building a gigantic ark in the middle of dry land. His neighbors must have thought he was out of his mind. Yet, Noah, trusting God's instructions, persisted in his task. He faced ridicule and doubt from those around him, but he did not let their disbelief sway his faith in God.

Finally, after years of hard work, the ark was finished. God sent animals to Noah, two of every kind, just as He had promised. Then the rain started, soft at first, but soon it turned into a torrential downpour. Water sprang up from the ground, and the fountains of the deep burst forth. It rained for forty days and forty nights, and the entire earth was covered in water.

Noah, his family, and the animals were safe inside the ark, riding out the storm. When the rain finally stopped, they waited for the water to recede. It was a long wait—almost a year. But at last, the day came when God told Noah to come out of the ark. The flood was over.

Noah's first act after stepping onto dry land was to build an altar to God. He thanked God for saving him and his family, and God made a promise, symbolized by a rainbow, never to destroy the Earth by a flood again.

From this story, we learn the importance of listening to God, even when others doubt us. Noah was likely ridiculed and doubted by those around him, but he remained faithful and obedient to God. His faith saved him and his family from the great flood.

We also learn from Noah the significance of patience and gratitude. Noah waited patiently for the storm to pass and for the waters to recede. And when it was finally over, his first act was one of gratitude towards God.

In our own lives, we may face situations where we feel called to take a step of faith that others might not understand. In these moments, let's remember Noah. Let's trust in God's plan, stay strong in our faith, and persist, even when others doubt us. And when we make it through the storm, let's remember to give thanks, just like Noah.

CHAPTER 27

THE DREAM VISION: JACOB'S LADDER

Jacob's dream of a ladder reaching heaven teaches us about God's continual presence and care.

Genesis 28:10-22

Have you ever had a dream that felt so real, so vivid, that it stuck with you long after you woke up? Well, Jacob, the grandson of Abraham, had a dream like that, and it changed his life.

Jacob was on the run from his brother, Esau, whom he had tricked out of his birthright and his father's blessing. Fearing his brother's wrath, Jacob fled, traveling alone with nothing but a staff in his hand. Tired and with nowhere to go, he chose a place in the wilderness to sleep for the night, using a stone as a pillow.

That night, he had a dream that was more than just a dream. In it, he saw a ladder set up on the earth with its top reaching the heavens. And there were angels, God's messengers, going up and down on it.

As if that wasn't enough, God Himself appeared to Jacob in the dream. He renewed the promise He had made to Abraham, saying that the land where Jacob was lying would be given to him and his descendants. He also promised that through his offspring, all families of the earth would be blessed.

But it wasn't just the promise that was significant. God also told Jacob, "Know that I am with you and will keep you wherever you go, and will bring you back to this land; for I will not leave you until I have done what I have promised you."

When Jacob woke up, he realized that he had encountered God in a powerful way. He took the stone he had used as a pillow, set it up as a pillar, and poured oil on top of it as an act of worship. He named the place Bethel, which means "House of God."

From this story, we learn about God's continual presence and care. Jacob was alone and on the run, but God was with him. The ladder in his dream was a symbol of the connection between heaven and earth, a reminder that God was not distant or detached. He was actively involved in Jacob's life, guiding him and promising to be with him.

So remember, even when you feel alone or afraid, God is with you. Like Jacob, you may encounter God in unexpected places and in unexpected ways. And even when you mess up, God's promises still stand. He cares for you, watches over you, and has a plan for your life. Just as He did with Jacob, God can turn even the most difficult situations into a pathway to His blessings.

CHAPTER 28

TWIN RIVALRY: ESAU AND JACOB

The story of Esau and Jacob shows us the impact of deceit and the power of reconciliation.

Genesis 25:19-34

In the annals of sibling rivalries, few are as intense as the one between Esau and Jacob. These two were twins, but they were as different as night and day.

Esau was a hunter, a man of the fields, and his father Isaac's favorite. Jacob was more of a homebody, preferring to stay close to the tents, and he was loved more by his mother, Rebekah.

From their birth, they were at odds. Esau was born first, but Jacob followed so closely that he was holding onto Esau's heel. The rivalry only intensified as they grew older.

One day, when Esau returned home exhausted and hungry from hunting, he found Jacob cooking a stew. Esau asked for some, but Jacob, ever the opportunist, asked him to sell his birthright in exchange. In his hunger, Esau agreed, showing little regard for the rights and responsibilities that came with being the firstborn.

But the real trouble started when their father, Isaac, was old and blind. He asked Esau to go hunting and prepare him a meal so that he could bless him. But Rebekah overheard and hatched a plan. She helped Jacob disguise himself as Esau, tricking Isaac into giving him the blessing that was meant for Esau.

When Esau found out, he was furious and vowed to kill Jacob. Fearful for Jacob's life, Rebekah sent him away to live with her brother Laban. Esau was left feeling cheated and robbed of his rightful place.

Years passed, and Jacob, after experiencing his own share of ups and downs, decided to return home. Fearing Esau's anger, he sent gifts ahead and prayed to God for protection. As he waited for Esau's arrival, he wrestled with God, receiving a new name, Israel, and a blessing.

When the brothers finally met, something unexpected happened. Instead of the revenge Jacob feared, Esau ran to meet him, embraced him, fell on his neck, and kissed him. They both wept, their old rivalry forgotten in the face of reunion.

From this story, we learn about the negative effects of deceit and the power of reconciliation. Jacob's tricks led to years of separation from his family and fear of reprisal. It was only when he returned home, ready to face the consequences, that he found forgiveness and reconciliation.

So remember, deception might offer temporary gains, but it also brings pain and separation. On the other hand, honesty, forgiveness, and reconciliation can heal old wounds and restore relationships. No matter how deep the hurt, with time, understanding, and a willingness to forgive, reconciliation is possible. Like Esau and Jacob, we can choose to let go of past hurts and embrace a future of peace and unity.

CHAPTER 29

The Ultimate Betrayal: Joseph and His Brothers

Joseph's journey from being sold into slavery by his jealous brothers to becoming a powerful leader in Egypt.

Genesis 37

Once upon a time, in the land of Canaan, there lived a young boy named Joseph. He was the eleventh of twelve sons and was his father Jacob's favorite. This favoritism, evident in the beautiful coat of many colors that Jacob gave to Joseph, stirred jealousy among his brothers.

Joseph also had the ability to interpret dreams, a gift from God that set him apart even more. When he shared his dreams—ones that suggested his family would one day bow down to him—his brothers' jealousy turned into resentment.

Their resentment eventually boiled over. One day when Joseph was sent by his father to check on his brothers, they seized the opportunity to get rid of him. They stripped Joseph of his coat, threw him into a pit, and then sold him into slavery to a caravan of Midianites heading to Egypt.

Back home, they dipped Joseph's coat in goat's blood and showed it to Jacob, who believed that a wild animal had killed his beloved son. Meanwhile, Joseph, now a slave, was taken to Egypt and sold to Potipar, the captain of Pharaoh's guard.

Despite the grim circumstances, Joseph did not lose hope or his faith in God. He worked diligently and earned Potipar's trust. However, a false accusation from Potipar's wife landed him in prison.

Even in prison, Joseph's faith remained steadfast. He continued to use his gift of interpreting dreams, which eventually caught the attention of Pharaoh himself. Joseph was brought before Pharaoh to interpret a troubling dream, which he revealed as a prophecy of seven years of abundance followed by seven years of severe famine. Impressed by Joseph's wisdom, Pharaoh appointed him as the second most powerful man in Egypt, tasked with preparing the nation for the coming famine.

Years later, when the famine hit, it affected not just Egypt but also Canaan, where Joseph's family lived. With no food, Joseph's brothers traveled to Egypt to buy grain, not knowing that they would have to negotiate with the brother they had sold into slavery years before.

Joseph recognized his brothers, but they did not recognize him. After testing them and seeing their remorse for their past actions, Joseph revealed his true identity. His brothers were terrified, expecting retaliation, but Joseph forgave them. He comforted his brothers, saying, "You intended to harm me, but God intended it for good to accomplish what is now being done, the saving of many lives."

In the end, Joseph's family moved to Egypt, where they were provided for and lived in peace. From a favorite son to a slave, from a prisoner to a ruler, Joseph's life was a rollercoaster of highs and lows.

From this story, we learn that even in the face of betrayal and hardship, we can choose to remain faithful and forgive those who wrong us. Joseph's brothers intended harm when they sold him into slavery, but God used it for good.

We may not always understand why we go through certain experiences, but we can trust that God can turn any situation around for good. When we face difficulties, let's remember Joseph's story and hold onto our faith, knowing that God is working things out for our good.

CHAPTER 30

A COAT OF MANY COLORS: THE FAVORITISM OF JOSEPH

Joseph's coat of many colors and the envy it sparked among his brothers teaches us about the harm of favoritism.

<u>Genesis 37:3-4</u>

In the ancient land of Canaan, a man named Jacob lived with his twelve sons. Among them, Joseph, the eleventh son, held a special place in Jacob's heart. Joseph was not just the firstborn of Rachel, Jacob's beloved wife, but he was also a boy of sterling qualities. He was handsome, intelligent, and possessed an innocence that made him a beloved son.

One day, Jacob decided to express his affection for Joseph in a way that turned out to be imprudent. He gifted Joseph a coat of many colors, a robe of remarkable beauty that was a symbol of honor and privilege. It was an extravagant gift, especially in a time and place where colors were often reserved for royalty. To Jacob, it was a perfect gift for his beloved son, but to his other sons, it was a blatant display of favoritism.

The coat instantly set Joseph apart from his brothers, causing a fissure in their already strained relationship. The brothers, older and laboring under the harsh sun, watched as Joseph, adorned in his vibrant coat, was excused from the grueling work. Their hearts churned with envy, and they could not speak peacefully to Joseph.

Adding to their resentment, Joseph had dreams that depicted his brothers, and even his parents, bowing to him. When he innocently shared these dreams, his brothers' envy turned into a burning hatred. The coat of many colors became a symbol of all that they despised— Joseph's favored status, his dreams, and their father's partiality.

Eventually, their jealousy boiled over. When they saw Joseph approaching from afar, his colorful coat making him easy to spot, they conspired to get rid of him. In a fit of anger and resentment, they seized Joseph, tore his cherished coat, and threw him into a pit. Later, they sold him as a slave to a caravan of Ishmaelites heading to Egypt.

They returned to their father with the coat, dipped in goat's blood, and claimed that a wild animal had devoured Joseph. The sight of the blood-soaked coat crushed Jacob. He mourned for his son in deep sorrow, refusing to be comforted, while his sons hid the bitter truth.

Joseph's story doesn't end in the pit, though. Despite his suffering, he rose to become a high-ranking official in Egypt, using his position to save many lives, including those of his brothers, during a severe famine. The brothers' malicious actions were used for good, leading to their eventual reconciliation.

This story serves as a powerful lesson about favoritism and its harmful effects. Favoritism breeds envy and discord, as seen in the animosity of Joseph's brothers. It disrupts harmony, causing rifts even in close-knit families. As parents, leaders, or individuals with influence over others, it's crucial to treat those under our care with fairness and equality.

Moreover, Joseph's story is a reminder of God's sovereignty. Even in the midst of the dire consequences of favoritism, God was able to bring about good. He used Joseph, the favored son, to save many lives, demonstrating that even when humans fail, God can turn the situation around for good.

Ultimately, the story teaches us to be aware of our actions and the potential consequences, especially when showing favoritism. It prompts us to promote fairness and equality in all our relationships, maintaining harmony, and reflecting God's love to all.

CHAPTER 31

THE LOYAL HELPER: THE STORY OF REBEKAH AT THE WELL

Rebekah's act of kindness to a stranger at a well teaches us about hospitality and the importance of helping others.

Genesis 24

Once upon a time, in a land far, far away, there was a young woman named Rebekah. You might be thinking that this is just another typical story about an ordinary girl from the past, but Rebekah was anything but ordinary. And what set her apart was not her beauty or her status but her generous heart and willingness to help others.

The story unfolds with a man named Abraham sending his trusted servant on a mission. This wasn't just any task – the servant was to find a suitable wife for Abraham's son, Isaac, and he was to look in Abraham's homeland, a place far away from where they were living.

The servant set off on his journey, and after traveling for months, he arrived at a well in the town of Nahor, exhausted and thirsty. He made a prayer, asking for God's guidance in finding the right woman for Isaac. He asked that the woman whom he was to choose would not only provide him with water when he asked but would also offer to water his camels.

As the servant finished his prayer, a beautiful young woman named Rebekah came to the well. The servant asked her for a drink, and to his surprise, she quickly agreed. Not only did she give him water, but she also offered to draw water for his camels, just as he had prayed for.

Can you imagine the shock on the servant's face when he realized that his prayer had been answered so precisely and quickly? Rebekah didn't know the servant or why he was there, yet she offered her help without expecting anything in return.

Impressed by her kindness and the way his prayer had been answered, the servant revealed his mission and asked Rebekah's family for her hand in marriage to Isaac. They agreed, and Rebekah, showing her courageous spirit, decided to leave her home and family to start a new life with Isaac.

Now, you may be wondering what makes this story relevant to you, right? You don't live near a well, and you're not about to set off on a camel journey. But what you can do is follow Rebekah's example of kindness and generosity.

Rebekah's story shows us that a simple act of kindness can make a big difference in someone's life. We never know when we're part of someone else's journey, and by showing a bit of compassion, we can change their path for the better. It's about helping out when we can, even if the person is a stranger, and doing so without expecting anything in return.

Her story also reminds us to have the courage to step into the unknown. Rebekah was willing to leave everything familiar to embark on a new journey, much like we sometimes have to do when starting a new school, moving to a new city, or even making new friends.

So, let's take a page from Rebekah's book and be kind to those around us. After all, we could be the answer to someone's prayer, just as Rebekah was to Abraham's servant.

CHAPTER 32

THE ULTIMATE SACRIFICE: ABRAHAM AND ISAAC

Abraham's willingness to sacrifice his beloved son, Isaac, teaches us about faith and obedience.

Genesis 22:1-19

Abraham was a man of extraordinary faith. He had left his homeland at God's command and had been given a son, Isaac, in his old age as God had promised. Isaac was the joy of Abraham's life, the embodiment of God's promise to make him a great nation.

One day, God tested Abraham's faith in a way that would shake any parent to their core. He instructed Abraham to take his beloved son Isaac and sacrifice him on a mountain that God would show him. It was a task that seemed to contradict God's earlier promise to make Isaac the bearer of Abraham's lineage.

Despite the anguish it must have caused him, Abraham chose to obey. He prepared for the journey, took Isaac, and set out for the mountain. As they walked, Isaac noticed that they had fire and wood but no lamb for the sacrifice. Abraham replied, "God himself will provide the lamb for the burnt offering, my Son."

When they reached the place God had told him about, Abraham built an altar and arranged the wood. He bound Isaac, laid him on the altar, and raised his knife. But just as he was about to strike, an angel called out from heaven, "Abraham! Abraham! Do not lay a hand on the boy. Do not do anything to him. Now I know that you fear God, because you have not withheld from me your son, your only son."

Abraham looked up and saw a ram caught by its horns in a thicket. He took the ram and sacrificed it instead of his son. Because of his obedience, God reaffirmed his promise to Abraham, blessing him and his descendants.

From this story, we learn about faith and obedience. Abraham's willingness to sacrifice Isaac is one of the most potent examples of faith and obedience in the Bible. He trusted God completely, even when God's command seemed to contradict His promise.

There might be times when we don't understand why certain things are happening in our lives. We may face situations that test our faith, and we may feel confused or scared. In those moments, remember Abraham. His faith in God was unwavering, even when everything seemed against him. His story reminds us to trust in God's plan, even when we don't understand it.

Moreover, the story is a profound picture of the love God has for us. Just as Abraham was willing to sacrifice his beloved son, God was willing to sacrifice His only Son, Jesus, to save us. The ram that replaced Isaac on the altar foreshadowed Jesus, who would become the ultimate sacrifice for our sins.

So, in our journey of faith, let's strive to trust God as Abraham did, confident that God has a plan for us. And let's remember the depth of God's love for us, a love so vast that He gave His one and only Son so we could have eternal life.

CHAPTER 33

MOSES' BURNING BUSH ENCOUNTER: THE CALL TO LEAD

Moses' encounter with God in the form of a burning bush shows us that God can call anyone to do extraordinary things.

Exodus 3:1-14

Sometimes, extraordinary things happen in the most unexpected places. Picture this - you're in the middle of your daily routine when, out of nowhere, you get a call that changes your life forever. It might sound far-fetched, but this is exactly what happened to a man named Moses.

At this point in his life, Moses was living as a shepherd in the desert, far removed from the grandeur of Egyptian palaces where he had been raised. One day, as he was tending to his flock, he spotted something unusual: a bush was on fire, but it wasn't burning up. Intrigued, he decided to take a closer look.

As he approached the burning bush, he heard a voice calling out to him, "Moses! Moses!" It was God speaking directly to him from within the flames. Moses was in awe and a little frightened, responding, "Here I am."

God told Moses that He had seen the suffering of His people in Egypt and had chosen Moses to lead them to freedom. Now, you might be thinking, why Moses? He was just an ordinary shepherd living in the desert. But that's just it - God often calls ordinary people to do extraordinary things.

However, Moses wasn't so sure about this. He doubted himself, asking God, "Who am I that I should go to Pharaoh and bring the Israelites out of Egypt?" But God reassured him, saying, "I will be with you."

Despite this assurance, Moses was still worried. He was unsure that the Israelites would believe him and that he wouldn't know what to say. But God was patient, providing Moses with signs to show the Israelites and promising to help him speak and teach him what to say.

The encounter with the burning bush was a turning point in Moses' life. He went from being a humble shepherd to leading an entire nation to freedom. It wasn't an easy task, and Moses faced a lot of challenges along the way. But through it all, he had faith in God and in the call that he had received.

So, what does this mean for us? We may not encounter a burning bush, but we can be open to the unexpected ways God might speak to us. We, like Moses, may feel inadequate, unsure of our abilities, and afraid of what lies ahead. But from this story, we learn that it's not about our strength but about God's power working through us.

God can use anyone, including you, to do incredible things. You might feel like just an ordinary teen, but don't forget that Moses was just an ordinary shepherd when he was called to lead. It's not about who we are or what we can do but about who God is and what He can do through us.

So, keep your ears, eyes, and heart open. You never know when you might have your "burning bush" moment, an unexpected call to do something extraordinary. And when that call comes, remember Moses, trust in God, and step forward in faith. You might be surprised by what you can achieve.

CHAPTER 34

THE BIG ESCAPE: CROSSING THE RED SEA

The thrilling escape story of Moses leading the Israelites out of Egypt and across the Red Sea.

<u>Exodus 14</u>

Many centuries ago, in the land of Egypt, there lived a humble man named Moses. Born to an Israelite family but raised in the Pharaoh's palace, Moses had fled Egypt after standing up for his people. Now, after many years, he was back on a divine mission: to free the Israelites from the cruel bondage of the Egyptians.

When Moses first asked Pharaoh to let the Israelites go, the request was met with scorn and increased hardship for his people. But Moses, with his brother Aaron by his side, didn't give up. With God's power, they brought ten plagues upon the land of Egypt. Only after the tenth and most devastating plague did Pharaoh relent and free the Israelites.

Moses led his people out of Egypt, but their journey to freedom was just beginning. As they reached the edge of the Red Sea, they heard the thunderous sound of Pharaoh's army approaching. Pharaoh had changed his mind about freeing the Israelites and was coming to force them back into slavery.

With the sea in front of them and Pharaoh's army behind them, the Israelites panicked. "Was it because there were no graves in Egypt that you brought us to the desert to die?" they lamented to Moses. But Moses remained calm. "Do not be afraid," he reassured them. "Stand firm, and you will see the deliverance the Lord will bring you today."

Then, God gave Moses a command. "Raise your staff and stretch out your hand over the sea to divide the water so that the Israelites can go through the sea on dry ground." Trusting in God, Moses did as he was told. As he raised his staff, a strong wind blew, parting the sea and turning the seabed into dry land.

With the sea split in two, the Israelites started their trek across the seabed, walls of water towering on either side of them. It was a miraculous sight, one that only reinforced their faith in God's power.

Meanwhile, Pharaoh's army was closing in fast. Emboldened by the sight of the Israelites "trapped" between the sea walls, they pursued them into the parted sea. But their triumph was short-lived.

Once the last of the Israelites had crossed, God told Moses to stretch out his hand over the sea again. As Moses lowered his staff, the sea walls collapsed, swallowing Pharaoh's army whole. Not one of them survived.

Finally, the Israelites were safe. They celebrated their freedom and praised God for His mighty act of deliverance. The journey ahead was still long and full of challenges, but that day by the Red Sea, they saw firsthand the lengths God would go to protect them.

From this story, we learn the power of faith and the importance of following God's guidance, even when things look impossible. The Israelites were trapped between an advancing army and a vast sea, yet God made a way for them.

Like the Israelites, we might face situations in our lives that seem impossible to navigate. But remember, just as God made a way for the Israelites, He can also make a way for us. So when you find yourself at the edge of your own "Red Sea," hold onto your faith for there is no obstacle too big for God.

CHAPTER 35

FAITH IN THE WILDERNESS: THE ISRAELITES' 40-YEAR JOURNEY

Navigating 40 years in the desert, the Israelites transitioned from a mindset of slavery to faith-filled readiness for the Promised Land, illustrating the transformative power of challenges and enduring hope.

Exodus, Leviticus, Numbers, Deuteronomy (specifically Numbers 14 for disbelief)

In the wake of their miraculous escape from Egypt, the Israelites found themselves not on a direct route to the Promised Land but rather on a prolonged and winding journey through a vast desert. Led by Moses, a humble man chosen by God, they embarked on what would become a 40-year sojourn in the wilderness.

As days turned into weeks and weeks into years, the Israelites faced numerous challenges: scorching days, freezing nights, and the constant uncertainty of their next meal or drink. Yet with every obstacle, God's grace was evident. When they thirsted, water sprang from rocks. When they hungered, manna, a heavenly bread, covered the ground, and quails filled their camp.

Despite these miracles, the Israelites often wavered in their faith. Memories of Egypt, though marked by bondage, also held recollections of abundant food and the security of a familiar land. They grumbled against Moses and even yearned to return to their life of enslavement, doubting the promise of a land flowing with milk and honey.

God, in His wisdom, recognized that the journey was not just about reaching a destination but about transformation. The Israelites needed to shed the mindset of slavery and cultivate a spirit of trust and obedience. The desert, with its hardships, served as a crucible for their faith.

Throughout their wanderings, there were moments of profound revelation. At Mount Sinai, they received the Ten Commandments, a moral compass for their lives. There were also moments of despair, like when they crafted a golden calf, forsaking the God who had done so much for them.

Moses, ever the mediator, often stood between the people and God's wrath. He reminded the Israelites of their covenant and urged them to remain steadfast in their faith, even when the Promised Land seemed like a distant dream.

Finally, after four decades, a generation raised in the wilderness, stronger in faith and spirit, stood on the cusp of the Promised Land. While Moses, due to his own moments of doubt, would not enter with them, he climbed Mount Nebo, gazing upon the land his people would soon inhabit.

The story of the Israelites in the desert teaches us that journeys, especially those filled with challenges, are as much about inner transformation as they are about reaching a destination. The Israelites left Egypt physically, but it took 40 years to truly free their spirits from the chains of doubt and fear.

From this narrative, we're reminded that faith isn't just about believing when times are good, but holding onto hope when the path is uncertain. Like the Israelites, we may face our own "desert" periods, times of trial and testing. But with faith as our compass, we can navigate these challenges and emerge stronger, ready to step into the promises that await us.

CHAPTER 36

THE WALLS FALL DOWN: JOSHUA AND JERICHO

Joshua's leadership in the battle of Jericho teaches us about faith and perseverance in the face of overwhelming odds.

Joshua 6

After Moses' death, leadership of the Israelites fell to Joshua, a man known for his faith and courage. His task was formidable: to lead the people into the Promised Land, a land still occupied by powerful nations. One of the first obstacles they faced was the fortified city of Jericho with its massive walls thought to be impenetrable. Yet, Joshua and the Israelites were about to witness a miraculous victory that only God could orchestrate.

God gave Joshua strange instructions for the battle. There would be no conventional attack. Instead, for six days, the Israelites were to march around the city once each day, with seven priests carrying trumpets made from ram's horns in front of the Ark of the Covenant. On the seventh day, they were to march around the city seven times. The priests would then blow their trumpets, and all the people would shout as loud as they could.

These instructions must have seemed unusual, even bizarre, but Joshua obeyed. For six days, they marched and remained silent as instructed. On the seventh day, after marching around Jericho seven times, the trumpets were blown, the people shouted, and something extraordinary happened. The walls of Jericho collapsed. The Israelites charged straight into the city and conquered it, just as God had promised.

From this story, we learn about faith and perseverance in the face of overwhelming odds. The task given to Joshua and the Israelites wasn't easy. Marching around a fortified city and expecting its walls to crumble must have seemed like a foolish strategy. Yet, Joshua and the people did as they were instructed. Their obedience and faith in God's promise led to a miraculous victory.

The story of Joshua and Jericho also teaches us about the power of collective faith and unity. The Israelites worked together, following God's instructions. It wasn't the shout of one person that brought the walls down; it was the collective shout of all the people.

In our own lives, we may face "walls" or obstacles that seem impossible to overcome. It could be a personal struggle, a difficult exam, a challenging relationship, or any number of things. In these times, let's remember Joshua and the battle of Jericho. Let's remember that faith and obedience to God, even when His ways seem strange to us, can lead to incredible victories.

When we unite with others in faith and purpose, we can see God's power at work in even greater ways. Let's not be afraid to lean on our community, to work together, and to encourage each other in faith. As we face our own "Jericho," let's keep marching, keep trusting, and prepare for the walls to fall down.

CHAPTER 37

THE EPIC SHOWDOWN: DAVID AND GOLIATH

A classic underdog story of how a small shepherd boy, David, defeats a terrifying giant, Goliath, using his faith and a simple sling.

1 Samuel 17

In the land of Israel, there was a shepherd boy named David. He was the youngest of eight brothers, so his tasks often involved watching the family's flock of sheep. Despite his simple life, David was anything but ordinary. He was courageous, quick-witted, and deeply faithful. And, most importantly, David had an unshakable trust in God.

Meanwhile, in the neighboring Philistine camp, a giant named Goliath was causing quite a stir. He stood over nine feet tall and was a fearsome sight to behold. Decked out in heavy bronze armor, Goliath was a formidable warrior who struck fear into the hearts of even the bravest soldiers.

For forty days, Goliath taunted the Israelites, daring any man among them to fight him in one-on-one combat. "Choose a man and have him come down to me," he bellowed. "If he is able to fight and kill me, we will become your subjects; but if I overcome him and kill him, you will become our subjects and serve us."

The Israelites were terrified. None of them dared to challenge the giant. But when David heard Goliath's words, he was not afraid. Instead, he was incensed. "Who is this Philistine," he questioned, "that he should defy the armies of the living God?"

David volunteered to fight Goliath. The Israelite soldiers, including David's brothers, thought he was mad. Even King Saul doubted David, saying, "You are not able to go out against this Philistine and fight him; you are only a young man, and he has been a warrior from his youth."

But David was not deterred. He told Saul about the times he had protected his flock from lions and bears, and how he believed that the same God who delivered him from the paw of the lion and the bear would deliver him from the Philistine.

Seeing David's courage and faith, King Saul agreed to let him fight Goliath. Saul tried to give him his own armor to wear, but David was not used to them. Instead, he picked up five smooth stones from a brook and placed them in his shepherd's bag. With only his sling as a weapon and faith as his armor, David walked out to meet Goliath.

Goliath laughed when he saw David. "Am I a dog," he roared, "that you come at me with sticks?" But David was not intimidated. "You come against me with sword and spear and javelin," he called back, "but I come against you in the name of the Lord Almighty."

Then, with a swift, practiced motion, David reached into his bag, took out a stone, and slung it at Goliath. The stone hit Goliath right between the eyes, and the giant fell face down on the ground.

The Philistine army watched in shock as David triumphed over the giant Goliath. David's victory that day wasn't due to his strength or skill. It was his faith in God that won the battle.

From this story, we learn that no challenge is too great when we have faith. David was just a shepherd boy, not a trained soldier. But he had trust in God and the courage to act, which made him a giant slayer.

Remember, just like David, we can face our giants - whether they are fears, difficulties, or challenges. And when we put our trust in God and take that step of faith, we too can overcome any giant that stands in our way.

CHAPTER 38

FROM SHEPHERD TO KING: THE JOURNEY OF KING DAVID

David's transformation from a simple shepherd boy to the king of Israel shows us that God sees our potential, even when others don't.

1 Samuel 16 to 2 Samuel 5

Once upon a time, in the rolling hills of Bethlehem, a young boy named David spent his days tending his father's sheep. He was the youngest of eight brothers and was often overlooked by his family. But what they didn't see, God saw.

God had chosen a new king for Israel to replace King Saul, who had disobeyed Him. He sent the prophet Samuel to the house of Jesse, David's father, to anoint one of Jesse's sons as the future king. When Samuel saw David's older brothers, he assumed one of them would be the future king. But God had a different plan.

God told Samuel, "Do not consider his appearance or his height, for I have rejected him. The Lord does not look at the things people look at. People look at the outward appearance, but the Lord looks at the heart."

Eventually, David, who was out tending the sheep, was called in. When Samuel saw him, God said, "Rise and anoint him; this is the one." And so, David was anointed to be the future king of Israel, chosen by God, not for his appearance or stature, but for his heart.

David's journey from shepherd to king wasn't instant. Before he became king, he faced Goliath, a giant who threatened his people. With faith and a sling, David defeated Goliath, proving that victory belongs to God.

Later, David found himself pursued by King Saul, who was jealous of David's popularity. Even then, David refused to harm Saul out of respect for his position as God's anointed king. David showed integrity, even in the face of danger.

After Saul's death, David was finally crowned king. As a king, David wasn't perfect. He sinned and faced the consequences of his actions. But throughout his life, he remained a man after God's own heart, humbly seeking forgiveness when he was wrong and praising God in times of joy.

From this story, we learn that God sees our potential, even when others don't. David was just a shepherd boy, overlooked by his own family. But God saw his heart and chose him to be king. Our worth is not determined by how others see us, but by how God sees us. He knows our hearts and our potential.

David's journey also teaches us about faith, courage, and integrity. He faced a giant with faith, fled from a jealous king with integrity, and led a nation with a heart devoted to God. We too can live with faith, courage, and integrity, knowing that God is with us, guiding our journey.

No matter where we are now, God has a plan for each of us. He sees our potential and has a purpose for our lives. And just like David, we can trust God, follow His ways, and let Him guide our steps. We may make mistakes along the way, but God's love for us is unwavering. With a heart open to God and a spirit willing to learn, we too can live lives that honor Him.

CHAPTER 39

A MOTHER'S LOVE: SOLOMON'S WISE DECISION

King Solomon's wisdom shines when deciding the true mother of a child, teaching us about justice and compassion.

1 Kings 3:16-28

King Solomon, the son of King David, was known far and wide for his wisdom. His ability to make fair and discerning judgments was admired by many, but there's one story in particular that really showcased his wisdom—the case of the two mothers.

The story goes like this. Two women, living in the same house, each had a newborn baby. One night, tragically, one of the babies died. The mother of the deceased child, stricken with grief, switched her dead infant with the other woman's living baby while she slept.

When the other woman woke up and saw the dead baby, she immediately knew it was not her own. But the other woman insisted that the living baby was hers. With no witnesses and no way to prove who the true mother was, they took the matter to King Solomon.

King Solomon listened to both women. Each claimed to be the mother of the living child and insisted that the dead baby belonged to the other. After careful consideration, Solomon proposed a solution. He called for a sword and declared that the living baby be cut in two, giving half to each woman.

The room must have fallen silent at this shocking suggestion. But then, the true mother of the living baby, filled with love for her child, cried out and pleaded with the king to give the baby to the other woman, just to save his life. The other woman, however, agreed to Solomon's solution.

Immediately, King Solomon knew who the real mother was. He gave the living baby to the woman who had shown willingness to give up her child rather than see him killed. His wise judgment not only revealed the truth but also preserved the life of the child.

From this story, we learn about justice and compassion. Solomon had a difficult decision to make, with no evidence to guide him. His wisdom guided him to propose a solution that revealed the truth. He understood that a true mother's love would choose the life and well-being of the child over anything else.

This story also teaches us about the importance of wisdom in decision-making. Solomon didn't rush his decision. He took the time to listen and understand the situation, and he used wisdom to discern the truth.

In our own lives, we may face difficult decisions and confusing situations. In such times, let's remember Solomon. Let's seek wisdom, listen well, and consider our options carefully. And as we make decisions, let's do so with justice and compassion, considering not only what is fair, but also what is kind and beneficial for everyone involved.

CHAPTER 40

UNEXPECTED FRIENDSHIP: RUTH AND NAOMI

A heartwarming story of loyalty and love between Ruth and her mother-in-law Naomi.

<u>*Ruth 1-4*</u>

In the small town of Bethlehem, a woman named Naomi lived with her husband and two sons. During a time of famine, they decided to leave their homeland and settle in the land of Moab. In Moab, her sons married two Moabite women, Ruth and Orpah. But over the next decade, Naomi experienced heart-wrenching loss as her husband and then her two sons died. She was left alone with her two daughters-in-law in a foreign land.

Hearing that the famine in Bethlehem was over, Naomi decided to return home. She urged her daughters-in-law to stay in Moab, find new husbands, and build a new life. Orpah, torn but eventually agreeing, decided to stay. But Ruth refused to leave Naomi's side.

Ruth spoke words of deep commitment to Naomi: "Don't urge me to leave you or to turn back from you. Where you go, I will go, and where you stay, I will stay. Your people will be my people and your God my God. Where you die, I will die, and there I will be buried."

So, Ruth and Naomi returned to Bethlehem. But life was hard for the two widows. They had to rely on the kindness of a relative of Naomi's husband, a man named Boaz, who allowed Ruth to gather grain from his fields.

Ruth worked tirelessly, day after day, gathering grain so she and Naomi could eat. Her dedication and her loyalty to Naomi did not go unnoticed. Boaz was impressed by Ruth's character and kindness. He ensured Ruth was protected and could gather plenty of grain.

As time went on, Boaz found himself drawn to Ruth's noble character, and Ruth found herself appreciating Boaz's kindness and respect. Eventually, Boaz married Ruth, securing a future for her and Naomi. Ruth, who had left her homeland and her people out of love for Naomi, was blessed with a loving husband and a son, securing her place in the lineage of King David and, ultimately, Jesus Christ.

From this story, we learn about the power of loyalty, love, and kindness. Ruth had every reason to leave Naomi and return to her own family in Moab. But she chose to stick with Naomi, showing extraordinary loyalty and love. Ruth's kindness and hard work also caught Boaz's attention, leading to her securing a future for herself and Naomi.

In our lives, we encounter people who need our loyalty and kindness, just like Naomi needed Ruth. And just like Ruth, we have the choice to show compassion and loyalty, to stick with them in difficult times. This story reminds us that our actions, guided by love and loyalty, can lead to unexpected blessings.

Furthermore, Ruth, a foreigner in a strange land, reminds us that everyone, regardless of their background or where they come from, has the potential to be a part of God's plan. God saw Ruth's heart, her faithfulness, and her love. He blessed her and used her in His grand design, demonstrating that God's love and purposes transcend boundaries of nation and ethnicity.

So, let's be like Ruth, embracing love, loyalty, and kindness, knowing that our actions can change not just our own lives, but the lives of those around us. And let's remember that no matter where we come from or what we've been through, God has a place for us in His plan.

CHAPTER 41

HANNAH'S HEARTFELT PRAYER: THE BIRTH OF SAMUEL

Hannah's persistent prayers for a child remind us of the power of prayer and God's timing.

<u>1 Samuel 1</u>

Imagine a woman whose heart longs for a child. Her days are filled with prayers, and her nights with silent tears. This is the story of Hannah, a woman who knew the agony of a barren womb, the sting of societal ridicule, and the yearning for a child she could call her own. But more than that, it is a story about the power of prayer and God's perfect timing.

Hannah was one of two wives of a man named Elkanah. His other wife, Peninnah, had been blessed with children, but Hannah had not. And Peninnah, seizing on this unfortunate circumstance, didn't miss an opportunity to taunt and belittle Hannah. This created an environment of tension and sorrow for Hannah, magnifying the void she already felt in her heart.

Each year, Elkanah's family would travel to the temple to worship and offer sacrifices to the Lord. And each year, as Hannah made her way to the temple, she carried a heavy heart burdened with longing. It was at the temple, one of these years, where Hannah's quiet despair turned into a fervent plea to God.

Hannah was alone in her pain, her heart echoing with emptiness. And it was in this quiet solitude that she began to pray, pouring out her heart to the Lord. This wasn't a polite, rehearsed prayer but a desperate, gut-wrenching plea. Hannah promised God that if He blessed her with a son, she would dedicate that child to Him for all the days of his life.

Eli, the priest, who was observing Hannah from a distance, misunderstood her silent prayers for drunken rambling. But when Hannah explained her sorrow and her promise to God, Eli blessed her and asked God to grant her petition.

This encounter with Eli seemed to strengthen Hannah. She left the temple with a renewed spirit, no longer sad. And in due course of time, God remembered Hannah. She conceived and gave birth to a son, whom she named Samuel, meaning "God has heard."

Hannah's joy must have been boundless. The son she had longed for was finally in her arms. But she did not forget her promise to God. Once Samuel was weaned, she took him to the temple and presented him to Eli.

And Samuel, the answered prayer, served God at the temple, under Eli's guidance, and went on to become one of Israel's greatest prophets.

The story of Hannah and Samuel speaks to us across the centuries, reminding us of several truths. First, it tells us that God hears our prayers. Hannah's fervent prayers were not lost on God. He heard her cry, He saw her heart, and in His perfect timing, He answered her prayer.

Second, it teaches us about patience. Hannah had to wait years before her prayers were answered. But her patient waiting is a testament to her faith. She trusted God, even when circumstances seemed bleak, and in her patient waiting, she was rewarded.

Finally, it underscores the importance of keeping our promises to God. Hannah promised to dedicate Samuel to God, and she kept that promise, even though it must have been difficult to leave her young son at the temple.

Like Hannah, we too might find ourselves in situations where we long for something. Our prayers might seem unanswered, our circumstances dire, and our hearts heavy. But let's remember that just as God heard Hannah's prayers, He hears ours too. Our timing might not align with His, but that does not mean He has forgotten us. His timing is perfect, and He knows what's best for us. Let's keep praying, keep trusting, and most importantly, let's keep our promises to God, knowing that He is faithful. Hannah's story assures us that God is always listening, and that with Him, even the deepest heartaches can turn into the greatest joys.

CHAPTER 42

AGAINST ALL ODDS: GIDEON'S SMALL ARMY

Gideon's victory with just 300 men proves that with God on our side, we can overcome any obstacle.

Judges 7

There was a time when the people of Israel were greatly oppressed by the Midianites. Year after year, the Midianites would invade the land, destroying crops and livestock, leaving the Israelites in a state of despair and poverty. During this difficult period, a man named Gideon was called by God to save his people.

Gideon was not a warrior. He was the least in his family, which belonged to the weakest clan in the tribe of Manasseh. Yet, God saw something in Gideon that he didn't see in himself. When God first called him, Gideon doubted that he was the right person for the task. He asked God for a sign, and God, in His patience, gave Gideon the reassurance he needed.

With newfound confidence, Gideon gathered an army of 32,000 men to fight against the Midianites. But God had a point to prove. He didn't want the Israelites to think that they won the battle by their own strength. So, He told Gideon to reduce his army.

Through a series of tests, Gideon's army was whittled down to just 300 men. These 300 men were up against a Midianite army that was as numerous as locusts with camels as countless as the sand on the seashore. It was an impossible match—a small group of 300 against an enormous army.

However, God gave Gideon a strategy. Each of the 300 men held a trumpet and a torch hidden in a jar. In the middle of the night, they surrounded the Midianite camp. At Gideon's signal, they blew their trumpets, broke the jars, and shouted, "For the Lord and for Gideon!" The Midianites, startled and confused, turned on each other. Gideon's small army didn't even need to fight— the enemy was defeated in their panic and chaos.

From this story, we learn that with God on our side, we can overcome any obstacle. Gideon's army was ridiculously outnumbered. In human terms, they stood no chance. But they were not relying on their own strength—they were relying on God. And with God, they turned the tide against an enemy that seemed unbeatable.

This story also teaches us about humility and faith. Gideon was not a likely hero. He was not strong, influential, or brave. But when God called him, he was willing to step out in faith. He recognized that the victory was not his, but God's.

In our own lives, we may feel like we're up against impossible odds. We might feel overwhelmed, outmatched, and out of our depth. But let's remember Gideon. Let's remember that it's not about our strength, but about God's. When we put our trust in Him, when we step out in faith and follow His lead, we can overcome any obstacle that stands in our way.

CHAPTER 43

SAMSON'S DOWNFALL: THE DANGER OF PRIDE AND DISOBEDIENCE

Samson's story is a stark reminder of how pride and disobedience can lead to our downfall.

Judges 16

In the book of Judges, nestled within the tumultuous narrative of Israel's cyclical rebellion and redemption, we find the story of Samson. Samson's life offers a stark portrayal of how unchecked pride and persistent disobedience can lead to disastrous consequences.

Samson's story begins even before his birth. An angel appears to his mother, a woman unable to bear children, announcing that she would give birth to a son. This son was to be a Nazirite, set apart for God, from the womb. He would begin to deliver Israel from the Philistines, their oppressors at that time.

Samson was blessed with extraordinary strength. However, his strength was not merely a physical attribute. It was deeply entwined with his dedication to God, symbolized by the uncut hair of his Nazirite vow. But from the beginning, we see signs of Samson's pride and self-will.

Despite being warned by his parents, Samson insists on marrying a Philistine woman, an act that goes against God's command for the Israelites not to intermarry with pagan nations. His pride and disobedience take hold, ignoring wise counsel and God's commands to satisfy his personal desires.

This decision leads to several violent confrontations with the Philistines, where Samson uses his divine strength not for God's purpose of delivering Israel, but to settle his personal scores. His exploits, while demonstrating his exceptional strength, also reveal his moral weaknesses and growing pride.

The turning point in Samson's life comes when he meets Delilah. The Philistine rulers bribe her to discover the source of Samson's strength. In an act of monumental folly, Samson, swayed by Delilah's persistent nagging and seduction, reveals his secret. His pride blinds him to the clear danger he is putting himself in.

When Delilah cuts off his hair as he sleeps, Samson's strength leaves him. The Philistines seize him, gouge out his eyes, and take him to Gaza, where he is made to grind grain in prison. His pride and disobedience have led to his downfall, reducing him from a mighty judge to a blind prisoner.

In prison, as his hair begins to grow back, Samson turns to God in repentance. His eyes, once blind to his pride and sin, are now physically blind but spiritually open. In his final act, he prays for God's strength to return to him one last time.

God hears his prayer. As Samson is brought out to entertain the Philistine rulers in their temple, he uses his restored strength to push apart the temple pillars. The temple collapses, killing him and the Philistines within, dealing a significant blow to Israel's oppressors.

Samson's story is a solemn reminder of the danger of pride and disobedience. Despite his divine calling and extraordinary gifts, his persistent disobedience and growing pride led to his downfall.

Moreover, it teaches us that our gifts and abilities, no matter how extraordinary, are not for our own glorification, but for God's purpose. When we use them guided by our pride and contrary to God's commandments, we set ourselves up for disaster.

Yet, even in his downfall, Samson's story offers hope. His final act of repentance shows that it's never too late to turn back to God. God, in His mercy, hears Samson's prayer and allows him to fulfill his divine purpose, albeit in a tragic manner.

Samson's life serves as a powerful reminder that we are not invincible, that our actions have consequences, and that persistent disobedience can lead to our downfall. But it also reminds us of God's mercy and the power of repentance, teaching us that even in our lowest points, turning back to God can lead to redemption.

CHAPTER 44

ELIJAH AND THE PROPHETS OF BAAL: A TEST OF FAITH

Elijah's showdown with the prophets of Baal shows us the power of unwavering faith.

1 Kings 18:20-40

In life, we often face situations that test our beliefs, push our limits, and challenge our faith. And in those moments, it can be hard to stay true to what we believe in. But imagine standing alone against 450 people, knowing that you're the only one defending the truth. Would you have the courage to stand your ground? This is the story of a man named Elijah who did just that.

Elijah was a prophet, someone who spoke God's words to the people. In his time, many people had turned away from God and were worshiping idols. The worst of these was Baal, a false god whom the Israelites were being led to worship by their wicked king, Ahab.

Distressed by his people's betrayal, God decided to show them who the real God was. So, He sent Elijah to challenge the prophets of Baal to a duel of sorts.

The challenge was simple. Both Elijah and the prophets of Baal would each prepare a bull for sacrifice and place it on an altar, but they wouldn't set it on fire. Instead, they would pray to their respective gods to send down fire from heaven to burn the sacrifice. The God who answered by fire would be recognized as the true God.

The prophets of Baal agreed to the challenge and went first. They called on Baal from morning until noon, dancing around the altar and even cutting themselves to get Baal's attention. But there was no response; no fire came down.

Then came Elijah's turn. He repaired the broken altar of God and prepared his bull. But he did something unexpected: he had four large jars of water poured over his offering, not once, not twice, but three times, until the sacrifice and the wood were thoroughly soaked, and a trench around the altar was filled with water.

Why would he do that, you might ask? Well, Elijah wanted to show that the miracle that was about to happen could only be the work of the almighty God.

Elijah then prayed, "Answer me, Lord, answer me, so these people will know that you, Lord, are God, and that you are turning their hearts back again."

And guess what happened? Fire fell from heaven and consumed the wet offering, the wood, the stones, the soil, and even evaporated the water in the trench.

The people who saw this were astounded and fell on their faces, declaring, "The Lord, He is God! The Lord, He is God!"

Elijah's showdown with the prophets of Baal is a powerful reminder of the strength of unwavering faith. Elijah was significantly outnumbered, but he stood his ground because he knew God was on his side.

From this story, we learn that no matter how daunting the odds seem, we should never compromise our beliefs. Just like Elijah, we can have the confidence to stand up for what's right, even when we feel like we're standing alone.

Remember, it's not about the number of people against you; it's about the One who is for you. Just like in Elijah's story, God is with you in your story too. So, hold onto your faith, even when it's tested. Stand up for what you believe in, and never forget the power of the One who stands with you.

CHAPTER 45

IN THE LIONS' DEN: THE COURAGE OF DANIEL

Daniel's unwavering faith in God, even when thrown into a den of hungry lions, inspires us to remain steadfast in our beliefs.

<u>Daniel 6</u>

In the kingdom of Babylon, there lived a man named Daniel. He was a Hebrew, taken from his homeland and brought to Babylon along with many others when King Nebuchadnezzar conquered Jerusalem. But Daniel wasn't just any captive. He was intelligent, wise, and above all, faithful to his God.

Daniel's wisdom quickly won him favor with the king, and he rose to a high position in the Babylonian court. He became one of the king's most trusted advisors, a position that made the other court officials quite envious.

As they plotted against Daniel, they realized that the only way they could find fault with him was concerning his faith. Daniel had a strict routine of praying to God three times a day, a practice that was well-known.

The officials convinced King Darius, who had taken over after Nebuchadnezzar, to issue a decree stating that for thirty days, anyone who prayed to any god or human except King Darius would be thrown into a den of lions. The king, unaware of the plot against Daniel, agreed and signed the decree into law.

Despite the decree, Daniel did not change his routine. He continued to pray to God three times a day, just as he always had. When the officials found Daniel praying, they reported him to the king, who was heartbroken but could not revoke his own law.

With a heavy heart, Darius ordered that Daniel be thrown into the lion's den, but not before saying, "May your God, whom you serve continually, rescue you!"

As night fell, Daniel found himself in the lion's den. But he was not afraid. He trusted God completely. Meanwhile, King Darius spent a sleepless night worrying about Daniel.

At the first light of dawn, Darius rushed to the lion's den. He called out, "Daniel, servant of the living God, has your God, whom you serve continually, been able to rescue you from the lions?"

To his great relief, he heard Daniel's voice respond, "May the king live forever! My God sent his angel, and he shut the mouths of the lions. They have not hurt me."

Hearing this, Darius was overjoyed. He ordered that Daniel be lifted out of the den. Daniel emerged unscathed, without a single scratch, for he had trusted in his God. The king then issued a decree that everyone in his kingdom must fear and reverence the God of Daniel, for He is the living God who rescues and saves.

From this story, we learn the importance of staying true to our beliefs, even when faced with dire consequences. Daniel knew that praying to his God could cost him his life, yet he chose to stand by his faith.

We too might face situations where our faith is challenged, where it might seem easier to hide our beliefs than stand up for them. But Daniel's story reminds us that staying true to our faith is worth it. Just as God protected Daniel, He will also be with us when we face our own "lion's dens."

CHAPTER 46

DEFYING THE KING: SHADRACH, MESHACH, AND ABEDNEGO

*The tale of three friends who refuse to compromise their beliefs,
even when threatened with a fiery furnace.*

<u>*Daniel 3*</u>

In the heart of the Babylonian kingdom, three friends - Shadrach, Meshach, and Abednego, stood out among the rest. Like Daniel, they were Hebrews brought to Babylon when King Nebuchadnezzar conquered Jerusalem. They were known for their intelligence, integrity, and unwavering faith in God.

King Nebuchadnezzar built a massive gold statue and issued a decree: as soon as the sound of music was heard, everyone was to fall down and worship the statue. Whoever didn't comply would be thrown into a blazing furnace.

Despite the threat of the furnace, Shadrach, Meshach, and Abednego refused to bow to the golden statue. Their devotion was to the God of Israel alone.

Their defiance quickly reached the ears of the king. Furious, Nebuchadnezzar summoned them and gave them one more chance to bow to the statue. Their response was one of absolute faith: "O Nebuchadnezzar, we do not need to defend ourselves before you in this matter. If we are thrown into the blazing furnace, the God we serve is able to save us from it, and He will rescue us from your hand, O king. But even if He does not, we want you to know, O king, that we will not serve your gods or worship the image of gold you have set up."

Outraged, Nebuchadnezzar ordered the furnace to be heated seven times hotter than usual. He then commanded his strongest soldiers to tie up Shadrach, Meshach, and Abednego and throw them into the blazing furnace.

As the king peered into the furnace, he was stunned by what he saw. Not only were the three friends unharmed, but they were also not alone. There was a fourth figure in the furnace, one "like a son of the gods." They were walking around in the fire, completely untouched by the flames.

Astounded, Nebuchadnezzar called them out of the furnace. When Shadrach, Meshach, and Abednego emerged from the fire, everyone saw that they were completely unharmed. Not a single hair on their heads was singed, their clothes were not scorched, and there was no smell of fire on them.

Moved by this miraculous event, Nebuchadnezzar declared, "Praise be to the God of Shadrach, Meshach, and Abednego, who has sent his angel and rescued his servants! They trusted in him and defied the king's command and were willing to give up their lives rather than serve or worship any god except their own God."

From this story, we learn the power of unwavering faith and the courage to stand up for our beliefs, even when faced with dire consequences. Shadrach, Meshach, and Abednego were willing to risk their lives rather than compromise their faith.

In our own lives, we might face pressure to compromise our values or beliefs. In those moments, remember the courage of these three friends. Their faith and trust in God saved them from the blazing furnace. And just as He was with them, God will be with us, protecting and guiding us when we stand up for our beliefs.

CHAPTER 47

THE RELUCTANT PROPHET: JONAH AND THE BIG FISH

Jonah learns the hard way that you can't run away from your responsibilities - or from giant fish.

<u>Jonah 1-4</u>

In the ancient lands of the Bible, a man named Jonah received a message from God. The city of Nineveh, known for its wickedness, needed a wake-up call, and Jonah was chosen to deliver it. But Jonah had other plans.

Rather than heading east to Nineveh, Jonah booked a ship going in the opposite direction. He thought he could escape God's presence, but he was soon proven wrong. A violent storm hit the sea, and the terrified sailors feared they would drown.

Jonah knew he was the cause of the storm. Feeling guilty, he suggested that the sailors throw him overboard to calm the sea. Reluctantly, they did as Jonah said, and the storm ceased immediately.

But Jonah's story was far from over. As he sank into the deep, a giant fish, sent by God, swallowed Jonah whole. He found himself in the belly of the fish, where he would spend the next three days and three nights.

In the depths of despair, Jonah cried out to God. He admitted his disobedience and begged for mercy. After three days, God commanded the fish to spit Jonah out onto dry land.

God gave Jonah a second chance to fulfill his mission. This time, Jonah went to Nineveh. He warned the people of their impending destruction unless they repented and turned away from their wicked ways. To Jonah's surprise, the Ninevites listened. From the greatest to the least, they turned away from their evil deeds, and God spared their city.

From this story, we learn that running away from our responsibilities only leads to more trouble. Jonah tried to escape his duty, but his actions caused a storm and got him swallowed by a big fish. Yet when he owned up to his mistakes and asked for forgiveness, God gave him a second chance.

We might not end up in the belly of a giant fish, but we can find ourselves in challenging situations when we try to dodge our responsibilities. The tale of Jonah and the big fish reminds us to face our tasks head-on, trusting in God's guidance. And even when we mess up, it's never too late to turn things around. With a sincere heart and a humble spirit, we can seek forgiveness and make things right again.

CHAPTER 48

THE UNEXPECTED HERO: QUEEN ESTHER'S BRAVERY

Esther's story of risking her life to save her people shows the power of courage and determination.

Esther 4-7

In the grand Persian Empire, a Jewish orphan named Esther became queen through a series of unlikely events. Esther was beautiful and kind, raised by her loving cousin Mordecai who served in King Xerxes's palace. But no one in the palace knew about Esther's Jewish heritage, as Mordecai had advised her to keep it a secret.

One day, a man named Haman was promoted by King Xerxes and given a high position in the kingdom. Everyone in the palace was required to bow to him, but Mordecai refused. This enraged Haman, and when he found out that Mordecai was a Jew, he decided not just to punish Mordecai, but to annihilate all the Jews in the kingdom.

Haman convinced King Xerxes to issue a decree that all Jews in the empire would be killed on a certain day. When Mordecai heard about this, he was devastated. He sent a message to Esther, urging her to use her position to save her people.

Esther was terrified. She knew that going to the king without being summoned could lead to her death. However, Mordecai urged her not to remain silent, saying, "Who knows but that you have come to your royal position for such a time as this?"

Faced with this challenge, Esther decided to risk her life to save her people. She asked all the Jews in the city to fast and pray for three days, and she did the same. Then, she put on her royal robes and approached King Xerxes.

When the king saw Esther, he was pleased and extended his gold scepter, a sign that she was spared. Esther invited the king and Haman to a banquet she had prepared. At the banquet, she revealed her Jewish identity and told the king about Haman's plot to kill her people.

Shocked and enraged, King Xerxes ordered Haman to be executed. He then gave Esther and Mordecai the authority to issue a new decree, allowing the Jews to defend themselves against their enemies. On the day intended for their destruction, the Jews prevailed over those who sought to harm them.

From this story, we learn about the power of courage and determination. Esther was an orphan, a Jew, and a woman in a time and place where all three could have limited her influence. Yet she did not let fear hold her back. She used her position as queen to save her people, showing remarkable bravery.

Like Esther, we may face situations that call for courage and determination. We might feel scared or unsure but remember that we are never alone. Just as God was with Esther, guiding and protecting her, He is also with us. We have been placed in our unique situations for a reason. So let's find our courage, stand up for what's right, and be the heroes of our own stories.

CHAPTER 49

EZEKIEL'S DRY BONES: HOPE IN HOPELESS SITUATIONS

Ezekiel's vision of dry bones coming to life shows us that with God, there is always hope, even in seemingly hopeless situations.

Ezekiel 37:1-14

Located in the heart of the Old Testament, Ezekiel's prophecies often transport us to surreal scenes, images woven together with divine symbolism. Among these visions, the valley of dry bones in chapter 37 stands out as a beacon of hope in the face of utter despair.

Ezekiel, both a prophet and a priest, found himself among the exiles by the Kebar River in Babylon, far from their homeland. The people of Judah were crushed in spirit, their hope drained by defeat and displacement. It's against this backdrop that God gives Ezekiel a vision - a valley filled with dry bones.

God's Spirit brings Ezekiel to a valley, an open expanse filled with countless dry bones scattered across the ground. These bones, bleached by the sun and stripped by the wind, were very dry, signaling that they had been there for a long time. This image painted a grim picture of utter lifelessness, a desolate scene of hopelessness and despair.

The Lord poses a question to Ezekiel, "Son of man, can these bones live?" Humanly speaking, the answer seems clear: these bones, void of life for so long, cannot live. They represent a situation beyond hope.

But Ezekiel responds, "O Sovereign Lord, you alone know."

God commands Ezekiel to prophesy to these bones, to declare the word of the Lord to this valley of death. As Ezekiel obeys, a rattling sound echoes through the valley. The bones start moving, each bone finding its mate, forming complete skeletons. Sinews form, then flesh, and finally, skin covers them. Yet, there was no breath in them - bodies formed, yet lifeless.

God then instructs Ezekiel to prophesy to the wind, to call upon the breath from the four winds to breathe life into these bodies. As Ezekiel prophesies, breath enters them, and they stand up - a vast army resurrected from dry bones. The vision ends with God's promise to restore Israel, to open their graves of exile, and bring them back to their land, filling them with His Spirit.

This vision wasn't just about dry bones in a valley; it symbolized the despairing exiles, believing they were cut off entirely, their hope lost, and themselves saying, "Our bones are dried up and our hope is gone; we are cut off." The dry bones represented their current hopeless situation.

Yet, God was using this dramatic vision to show His people, and us, that no situation is beyond His reach. Just as He could breathe life into a valley of dry bones, He could restore His people, breathe life into their despair, and resurrect their hope. The lifeless bones, resurrected as a vast army, demonstrated that God could bring hope and restoration out of the most hopeless situations.

The story of Ezekiel's dry bones teaches us that no matter how dire, how hopeless, or how lifeless a situation may seem, it's never beyond God's power to restore. When all hope seems lost, when dreams have faded, and when life seems like a valley of dry bones, God can breathe new life and resurrect hope.

As we face our valleys of dry bones - those areas in our lives that seem void of hope - let us remember Ezekiel's vision. Let's remember that our God specializes in impossible situations, that He breathes life into the lifeless, and that He resurrects hope in the most hopeless situations. God's restorative power knows no bounds, and with Him, there's always hope.

CHAPTER 50

Nehemiah Rebuilds the Wall: Perseverance in the Face of Opposition

Nehemiah's dedication to rebuilding Jerusalem's walls, despite opposition, teaches us about determination and trusting in God.

Nehemiah 1-6

Nehemiah, a Jewish man serving as cupbearer to King Artaxerxes of Persia, is an enduring testament to what can be achieved with faith and perseverance. His life's story is a compelling narrative of relentless determination, dogged courage, and absolute trust in God, as he takes on the mammoth task of rebuilding the walls of Jerusalem amidst formidable opposition.

The first glimpse we have of Nehemiah is of a man expressing sorrow over the news that the walls of Jerusalem lay in ruin and its gates had been burned. As a result, the city, symbolic of their national and religious identity, was vulnerable to enemy attacks. Nehemiah's reaction to this devastating news was to pray, displaying his deep faith and reliance on God.

His prayer wasn't a mere whisper of wishful thinking. Nehemiah's prayer was a heartfelt plea, filled with confession, worship, and specific requests. It was a prayer that revealed his understanding of God's promises to Israel. Armed with this prayer, Nehemiah made a bold request to King Artaxerxes to allow him to return to Jerusalem and rebuild its walls.

With the king's permission and protection, Nehemiah embarked on his journey back to his ancestral home. Upon arrival, he secretly inspected the ruined walls under the cover of night, sizing up the monumental task before him. The walls that once echoed with the prayers of prophets and kings now lay silent, a haunting reminder of past glory. However, Nehemiah saw not just the crumbled stones but the possibility of restoration.

He rallied the people of Jerusalem with a stirring speech, motivating them with the promises of God and the backing of King Artaxerxes. The people responded with enthusiasm, declaring, "Let us start rebuilding." Work on the wall began, with each family working diligently on a section.

But the task wasn't without opposition. Nehemiah and his workers faced threats and ridicule from local officials Sanballat, Tobiah, and Geshem. The workers, armed for battle while laboring on the walls, persevered through these challenges. Nehemiah's leadership shone through as he addressed their fears and uncertainties, continually pointing them to trust in God.

Despite a series of plots to discourage and threaten them, Nehemiah and the workers remained undeterred. The work on the wall progressed steadily, with each stone set a testament to their unwavering faith and determination. In a mere fifty-two days, a task that seemed almost insurmountable was accomplished. The walls of Jerusalem stood tall once again, the gates were in place, and a sense of security restored.

Nehemiah's story is a profound lesson in perseverance and faith in the face of opposition. It shows us that with God-given vision and purpose, coupled with unwavering faith and determination, seemingly impossible tasks can be achieved.

As we face our challenges, let's remember Nehemiah rebuilding the walls of Jerusalem. May his story remind us to turn to God in prayer, stay focused on the task at hand despite opposition, and trust in God's promises. Like the walls of Jerusalem rising from the rubble, we can also see restoration and completion in our lives. Nehemiah's story is an enduring symbol of hope and resilience, demonstrating that with God, perseverance in the face of opposition can lead to significant accomplishments.

⭐⭐⭐⭐⭐

A QUICK REVIEW HELPS
MORE THAN YOU KNOW!

BE A BEACON! Your review contributes to our goal to reach more readers and help others find their way. **It only takes 20 seconds!**

Made in the USA
Coppell, TX
06 December 2024

41896268R00098